MAPLE AND BRICK

A STORY OF TRANSFORMATION IN A SMALL-TOWN FACTORY

DAVID S. MORGAN

Copyright © 2024 by David S. Morgan

All rights are reserved, and no part of this publication may be reproduced, distributed, or transmitted in any manner, whether through photocopying, recording, or any other electronic or mechanical methods, without the explicit prior written permission of the publisher. This restriction applies to any form or means of reproduction or distribution.

Exceptions to this rule include brief quotations that may be incorporated into critical reviews, as well as certain other noncommercial uses that are allowed by copyright law. Any such usage must adhere to the specified conditions and permissions outlined by the copyright holder.

Book Design by HMDPUBLISHING

CONTENTS

Preface ... 4
1. The Weight of Legacy ... 7
2. The Winds of Change ... 14
3. The Reluctant Hero ... 22
4. A Catalyst Arrives ... 29
5. Resistance and Doubt ... 36
6. The First Steps ... 44
7. Unearthing the Past ... 52
8. Allies and Adversaries ... 59
9. The Point of No Return ... 68
10. Crisis and Opportunity ... 76
11. The Dark Night of the Soul ... 84
12. Embracing Innovation ... 91
13. Trials and Tribulations ... 99
14. The Town's Awakening ... 107
15. A New Vision Emerges ... 114
16. Transformation in Action ... 121
17. The Final Test ... 129
18. Rebirth and Legacy ... 136
19. Epilogue ... 142
20. The Maple and Brick Way ... 145
21. The Blueprint ... 148

PREFACE

In the heart of America, countless small towns are anchored by factories that have stood for generations. These bastions of industry have weathered economic storms, technological revolutions, and shifting cultural tides. Yet, in recent decades, many have found themselves at a crossroads, facing the urgent need for transformation or the risk of obsolescence.

"Maple and Brick: A Story of Transformation in a Small-Town Factory" is a fictional account that captures this pivotal moment. While the town and its factory are products of imagination, the challenges, struggles, and triumphs depicted within these pages are very real, drawn from my decades of experience in the manufacturing world.

As an engineer, supervisor, and manager, I witnessed firsthand the resistance to change that often calcifies in long-established institutions. Later, as a consultant and CEO, I had the privilege of guiding various businesses—both for-profit and nonprofit, across a spectrum of industries; semiconductor equipment, CNC vertical machining centers, plastics and investment casting, assistive technology, and job shop machining, —through the tumultuous waters of process improvements, product innovation, and organizational transformation.

This book is a distillation of those experiences. It explores the human element of organizational change—the fear, the hope, the conflicts, and the breakthroughs. Through the story of Maple and Brick, readers will encounter familiar scenarios: the clash between tradition and progress, the struggle to adapt ingrained processes, and the delicate balance of preserving a company's soul while evolving its practices.

My aim in writing this book is twofold. First, to offer a compelling narrative that resonates with anyone who has ever been part of a changing organization. Second, to provide insights and strategies that readers can apply in their own professional lives, regardless of their industry or position.

"Maple and Brick" is for the manager seeking to lead change, the worker grappling with new realities, the entrepreneur looking to innovate, and anyone interested in the dynamics of organizational transformation. It is my hope that this story will not only entertain but also inspire and equip readers to become agents of positive change in their own workplaces and communities.

As you embark on this journey through Maple and Brick, I invite you to reflect on your own experiences with change and to consider the role you might play in shaping the future of your organization. After all, the story of transformation is not just about factories or businesses—it's about people, and the remarkable things we can achieve when we embrace the challenge of change.

It's important to acknowledge that this short book cannot do full justice to the wide range of voices and employee challenges present in real-world transformations. "Maple and Brick" offers but one small glimpse, a slice of the myriad challenges and opportunities that individuals and organizations face during periods of change.

Moreover, it's crucial to recognize that organizational transformation can lead to varied outcomes. Some changes result in growth and prosperity, with companies expanding and hiring additional employees. Other organizations must transform in different ways, perhaps by rethinking their current model, changing processes, or streamlining operations. These latter transformations, while necessary for survival and future success, may not always lead to immediate growth in terms of workforce or revenue.

This book aims to explore both types of transformations, acknowledging that the path to organizational health and sustainability isn't always straightforward or universally positive in the short term. It seeks to honestly portray the complex realities that businesses face in adapting to new market conditions, technological shifts, or economic pressures.

As you embark on this journey through Maple and Brick, I invite you to reflect on your own experiences with change and to consider the various forms that successful transformation might take. Consider how the scenarios presented might differ or align with your own encounters with organizational transformation. After all, the story of transformation is not just about factories or businesses—it's about people, and the remarkable things we can achieve when we embrace the challenge of change, whatever form it may take.

David S. Morgan

CHAPTER 1:
THE WEIGHT OF LEGACY

The old maple tree stood sentinel at the entrance of Maple and Brick Manufacturing, its gnarled branches reaching skyward like arthritic fingers grasping for hope. Bob Harrington, CEO of the struggling company, paused beneath its shade, his gaze fixed on the weathered brick building beyond. The factory had been a cornerstone of Peterborough, New Hampshire, for generations, its history intertwined with that of the town and Bob's own family.

As the morning sun painted the sky in hues of pink and gold, Bob couldn't shake the feeling that he was standing at a crossroads. The company that his ancestors had built from nothing was now teetering on the brink of obsolescence. The weight of their legacy pressed down on his shoulders, a burden he wasn't sure he could bear.

He took a deep breath, inhaling the crisp autumn air tinged with the faint scent of machine oil that always seemed to linger around the factory. It was a smell that had been part of his life for as long as he could remember. As a child, he had played in the shadow of these brick walls, the rhythmic hum of machinery a constant lullaby. Now, that same hum seemed more like a death rattle.

Bob's mind drifted back to those childhood days. He remembered running through the factory floors, dodging between the legs of workers, the air thick with cotton fibers from the textile machines. His grandfather, stern-faced but with kind eyes, would scoop him up and sit him on his knee, explaining the intricate workings of each machine. "One day, Bobby," he'd say, "all of this will be yours to take care of. It's not just a factory, it's the heart of Peterborough."

Those words echoed in Bob's mind now, a reminder of the responsibility he carried. It wasn't just about profit margins and market share; it was about the soul of a community.

With a sigh, Bob pushed open the heavy wooden doors and stepped into the factory. The interior was a study in contrasts – gleaming modern equipment stood alongside machines that had been in use since his grandfather's time. It was a visual representation of the company's struggle to adapt to changing times while holding onto its roots.

The factory floor stretched out before him, a vast expanse of concrete and metal bathed in the harsh glow of fluorescent lights. To his left, the old textile looms still stood, silent sentinels of a bygone era. They hadn't been used in years, not since the company had pivoted to plastics and electronics in the 1960s, but Bob's father had never had the heart to remove them. To the right, injection molding machines hummed and whirred, spitting out plastic components for everything from car parts to consumer electronics.

"Morning, Mr. Harrington," called out Joe, the veteran machinist turned maintenance manager. His gruff voice carried over the din of the factory floor. Joe had been with the company for over four decades, a living embodiment of Maple and Brick's history. His calloused hands and oil-stained coveralls told the story of a lifetime spent tending to the machines that were the lifeblood of the factory.

"Morning, Joe," Bob replied, forcing a smile. "How are we looking today?"

Joe's weathered face creased with concern. "Well, sir, we've got that order for Aerodyne Systems that's behind schedule. Jacob's been working overtime trying to get the inventory sorted, but we're still having issues with the new digital system." He gestured towards the far end of the factory, where a cluster of computers had been set up. "If you ask me, we were better off with the old paper ledgers. At least those didn't crash."

Bob nodded, his stomach tightening. Aerodyne was one of their biggest clients, and they couldn't afford to lose them. "I'll check in with Jacob. Thanks, Joe."

As he made his way through the factory, Bob couldn't help but notice the worried glances exchanged by the workers. News of the company's troubles had spread, and the air was thick with uncertainty. He passed by the break room, overhearing snippets of conversation that made his heart sink.

"Did you hear about Millstone Manufacturing over in Keene? They just laid off half their workforce..."

"My cousin works at that new tech startup in Manchester. Says they're always hiring..."

"I don't know how much longer we can hold on here..."

He found Jacob, the young shipping supervisor, hunched over a computer terminal, his face a mask of frustration. "Jacob," Bob called out, "talk to me about this Aerodyne order."

Jacob looked up, dark circles under his eyes betraying his lack of sleep. "Mr. Harrington, I've been trying to get this sorted all night. The new inventory system keeps glitching, and I can't get an accurate count of our stock. I think we might be short on some key components."

Bob felt a headache building behind his eyes. The new digital inventory system had been his idea – an attempt to modernize their operations. But so far, it had caused more problems than it solved. "Alright, Jacob. Do what you can. If we need to, we'll go back to the old manual system for now. We can't afford to mess up this order."

As he turned to leave, Bob caught sight of Emily, the head of their fledgling R&D department, engaged in an animated discussion with her team. Her passion for sustainability and innovation had been a breath of fresh air when she joined the company two years ago. But translating her ideas into profitable products had proved challenging.

"Emily," he called out, "how's that new biodegradable polymer coming along?"

Emily's face lit up, her enthusiasm a stark contrast to the gloomy atmosphere that permeated the rest of the factory. "Oh, Mr. Harrington! We've made some really exciting progress. I think we might be close to a breakthrough that could revolutionize our product line. We've been running tests on a new compound that's not only fully biodegradable but also has improved tensile strength. It could be perfect for eco-friendly packaging, and I've been thinking about potential applications in the medical field too."

Bob nodded, trying to muster some enthusiasm. "That's great, Emily. But remember, we need solutions that are commercially viable. We can't afford to pour resources into projects that won't pay off in the short term."

He saw the light dim a little in Emily's eyes, and he felt a pang of guilt. He wanted to encourage innovation, but the reality of their financial situation weighed heavily on every decision. "Keep up the good work," he added, hoping to soften the blow. "Maybe we can sit down later this week and discuss how we might be able to fast-track some of these ideas to market."

As he continued his rounds, Bob found himself in front of a faded photograph hanging in the main corridor. It showed the factory as it had been in its heyday – a bustling center of industry, with smoke billowing from its chimneys and workers streaming in and out of its doors. In the foreground stood a man with a striking resemblance to Bob himself – his great-grandfather, Rhys Morgan.

Rhys had been the one to truly put Maple and Brick on the map, transforming it from a small local mill into a thriving manufacturing powerhouse. His innovations had seen the company through the Great Depression and two world wars. What would Rhys think of the company now, struggling to stay relevant in a rapidly changing world?

Bob's musings were interrupted by the arrival of Laura Mitchell, the head of sales and marketing. Her usually immaculate appearance was slightly disheveled, a sign of the stress they were all under.

"Bob, we need to talk," Laura said, her voice tight with concern. "I've just gotten off the phone with Aerodyne. They're threatening to pull their contract if we can't deliver on time and up to spec. We can't afford to lose them."

Bob felt the weight on his shoulders grow even heavier. "I know, Laura. I've just spoken to Jacob about it. We're doing everything we can."

Laura's eyes narrowed slightly. "With all due respect, Bob, 'everything we can' might not be enough anymore. We're losing market share every day to companies that are more agile, more innovative. We need to make some big changes, and fast."

"What do you suggest?" Bob asked, bracing himself for the answer.

Laura took a deep breath. "I think we need to consider outsourcing some of our production. There are factories in Asia that could produce our components at a fraction of the cost. It would allow us to be more competitive on price."

Bob felt as if he'd been punched in the gut. Outsourcing would mean layoffs, a devastating blow to the community that had supported Maple and Brick for generations. "That's... that's a big step, Laura. Let's consider all our options before we go down that road."

As the day wore on, Bob found himself back in his office, staring out the window at the town of Peterborough spread out below. The factory had once been the lifeblood of this community, providing jobs and stability for generations. Now, its future – and by extension, the future of the town – hung in the balance.

From his vantage point, he could see Grove Street and the Peterborough Town Library, the oldest free public library in the world supported by taxation. Its historic brick facade and welcoming atmosphere had been a cornerstone of the community since 1833. The diner was coming alive and he could see young people heading off to school. He thought about the high school down the road where Maple and Brick sponsored the robotics club and offered internships to promising students

His gaze fell on a small, framed piece of paper on his desk. It was a poem, written by his great-grandmother, Sarah Morgan. The words spoke of the pride and perseverance of the mill workers, of the strength found in the maple's shade and the brick's steadfast presence. It was a reminder of where they had come from, of the spirit that had built this company.

But was that spirit enough to save them now?

As the sun began to set, casting long shadows across the factory floor, Bob made a decision. He couldn't let Maple and Brick fade away, couldn't let down the generations that had come before him or the community that depended on them. Something had to change.

He picked up his phone and dialed a number he'd been avoiding for weeks. "Dr. Turner? This is Bob Harrington from Maple and Brick. I think... I think we need your help."

As he hung up the phone, Bob felt a mix of fear and determination. The winds of change were coming to Maple and Brick, whether they were ready or not. And it was up to him to navigate the storm.

He stood up, walking to the window once more. The lights of Peterborough twinkled in the gathering dusk, a constellation of lives and livelihoods tied to the fate of Maple and Brick. Bob placed his hand on the cool glass, as if reaching out to the town itself.

"I won't let you down," he whispered, to the town, to his ancestors, to the workers who depended on him. "We'll find a way through this. We have to."

With renewed resolve, Bob turned back to his desk. There was work to be done, hard decisions to be made. But for the first time in months, he felt a glimmer of hope. Maple and Brick had weathered storms before. With the right guidance, with the spirit of innovation that had built this company, they could do it again.

The journey ahead would be difficult, fraught with challenges and uncertainties. But as Bob looked out over the factory floor, at the machines that had been the heartbeat of this community for generations, he knew it was a journey worth taking.

The legacy of Maple and Brick was more than just bricks and mortar, more than balance sheets and profit margins. It was the story of a town, of generations of workers, of American ingenuity and perseverance. And Bob was determined to write the next chapter in that story, no matter what it took.

CHAPTER 1 REFLECTION: THE WEIGHT OF LEGACY

Key Insights:
- ❖ Legacy carries both the wisdom of the past and the weight of expectations.
- ❖ Balancing respect for tradition with the need for innovation is crucial for leadership.

Personal Reflection:

Think about a legacy you've inherited, whether in your personal life or professional career. How has this legacy shaped your decisions and actions? In what ways has it empowered you, and where might it be holding you back?

Application Question:

How can you honor the legacy you've been given while still paving the way for necessary growth and change in your life or organization?

Action Step:

Identify one aspect of your inherited legacy that you want to preserve and one that you believe needs to evolve. Write down specific actions you can take to achieve both.

Quote to Remember:

"We are not just preserving a company; we are carrying forward a legacy while forging a new path."

CHAPTER 2:
THE WINDS OF CHANGE

The following morning dawned crisp and clear, a stark contrast to the cloud of uncertainty hanging over Maple and Brick. Bob Harrington arrived at the factory earlier than usual, his mind racing with a mix of hope and apprehension about Dr. Turner's impending visit.

As he walked through the parking lot, Bob noticed a sleek electric vehicle pulling into a space near the entrance. A woman emerged, her posture confident and purposeful. Dr. Evelyn Turner had arrived.

"Dr. Turner," Bob called out, extending his hand. "Thank you for coming on such short notice."

Dr. Turner shook his hand firmly, her keen eyes taking in the factory behind him. "Please, call me Evelyn. And thank you for having me, Bob. I'm looking forward to getting to know Maple and Brick."

As they walked towards the entrance, Evelyn's gaze swept over the building's facade. "This facility has quite a history, doesn't it?" she remarked.

Bob nodded, a hint of pride in his voice. "Indeed. My grandfather started this company right after World War II. He went into the building that my ancestors built a textile business in the late 1800s. We've been a cornerstone of this community for decades."

"And now you're facing some challenges," Evelyn said, her tone matter-of-fact but not unkind. "Tell me, Bob, what do you see as the biggest obstacle to Maple and Brick's success right now?"

Bob hesitated, considering the question. "Honestly? It feels like everything is an obstacle. Falling productivity, rising costs, increasing customer demands, outdated equipment... Sometimes it seems like we're fighting fires on all fronts."

Evelyn nodded thoughtfully as they entered the building. "I understand. But let me ask you this: beneath all those symptoms, what do you think is the root cause?"

Before Bob could answer, they were interrupted by the arrival of Laura Mitchell, the head of sales and marketing. Laura's sharp suit and brisk manner contrasted sharply with the more casual attire of the factory workers around her.

"Bob, we need to talk," Laura said, her tone urgent. "Aerodyne Systems is threatening to pull their contract if we can't improve our quality control immediately. We can't afford to lose them."

Bob introduced Laura to Dr. Turner, explaining her role as a consultant. Laura's eyes narrowed slightly, a mix of curiosity and skepticism in her gaze.

"With all due respect, Dr. Turner," Laura said, "we need concrete solutions, not consultancy speak. Our competitors are eating our lunch, and we're bleeding market share."

Evelyn met Laura's gaze steadily. "I appreciate your concern, Ms. Mitchell. In my experience, lasting solutions come from a deep understanding of the entire system. That's what I'm here to develop. But I'd love to hear more about the challenges you're facing in sales and marketing. Perhaps we could chat later today?"

Laura seemed taken aback by Evelyn's direct approach. She nodded curtly before excusing herself, leaving Bob and Evelyn to continue their tour.

As they walked through the factory floor, Evelyn observed the operations closely, occasionally stopping to chat with workers or examine a piece of equipment. Bob watched in amazement as she effortlessly engaged with everyone from seasoned machinists to young interns, asking probing questions and listening intently to their responses.

They approached the molding department, where Emily was engrossed in discussion with her team. Bob made the introductions, and Emily's eyes lit up with recognition.

"Dr. Turner! I read your paper on integrating sustainability into manufacturing processes. It was incredibly insightful," Emily said enthusiastically.

Evelyn smiled warmly. "I'm glad you found it helpful, Emily. I'd love to hear about any sustainability initiatives you're working on here at Maple and Brick."

As Emily began to outline her ideas for recycling and eco-friendly materials, Bob noticed a spark in her eyes that he hadn't seen in months. Evelyn listened attentively, asking pointed questions that seemed to help Emily refine her thoughts in real-time.

"You know," Evelyn said thoughtfully, "your ideas about sustainability could do more than just reduce waste. They could be a key differentiator in the market, especially with your aerospace and medical clients. Have you considered how these initiatives might tie into your overall business strategy?"

Emily's brow furrowed. "Honestly, I've been so focused on the technical aspects, I haven't thought much about the broader business implications."

Evelyn nodded understandingly. "That's not uncommon. But bridging that gap between technical innovation and business strategy is often where the real magic happens. Perhaps we could explore that further?"

As they moved on, Bob marveled at how Evelyn had so quickly honed in on a potential opportunity that he had overlooked. He was beginning to see why her reputation in the industry was so strong.

Their next stop was the shipping department, where they found Jacob poring over a complex spreadsheet. He looked up as they approached, his expression a mix of excitement and nervousness.

"Mr. Harrington, I've finished the proposal we discussed yesterday," Jacob said, handing Bob a thick folder. "I've included cost projections, implementation timelines, and potential ROI scenarios."

Bob introduced Jacob to Evelyn, explaining his role and his ideas for improving inventory management. As Jacob began to outline his proposal, Evelyn listened intently, occasionally asking for clarification on specific points.

"Jacob, this is impressive work," Evelyn said when he had finished. "You clearly have a strong grasp of the technical aspects. But I'm curious -- have you considered how these changes might impact the workflow in other departments? Or how they might affect your suppliers?"

Jacob blinked, caught off guard. "I... I guess I haven't thought about that as much," he admitted.

Evelyn smiled encouragingly. "That's okay. Systems thinking can be challenging, especially when we're deeply focused on our own area of expertise. But considering those broader impacts and relationships is crucial for successful change implementation. Perhaps we could work together to expand this proposal to address those aspects?"

As they left Jacob to his work, Bob turned to Evelyn. "I have to say, I'm impressed. You've already identified connections and opportunities that I hadn't seen, and it's only been a few hours."

Evelyn's expression turned serious. "Bob, what I'm seeing here is a company with enormous potential. You have passionate, skilled people with great ideas. But there seems to be a disconnect -- between departments, between technical innovation and business strategy, between the company's rich history and its future potential."

They paused near the maintenance area, where Joe was demonstrating a complex repair procedure to a group of younger workers. Evelyn watched the interaction with interest.

"Take that scene, for instance," she said, nodding towards Joe. "There's a wealth of knowledge there, built up over decades. But is it being systematically captured and integrated into your processes? Or will it walk out the door when Joe retires?"

Bob felt a pang of guilt. They had talked about implementing a knowledge management system for years, but it had always been pushed to the back burner in favor of more immediate concerns.

"The good news," Evelyn continued, "is that these are all solvable problems. But it will require a shift in thinking -- from reactive to proactive, from siloed to integrated, from short-term fixes to long-term transformation."

She turned to face Bob directly. "You asked earlier about the root cause of Maple and Brick's challenges. Based on what I've seen today, I believe the core issue is not any specific process or market condition, but rather the company's overall approach to change and innovation. You've been so focused on keeping the ship afloat that you haven't had the chance to chart a new course."

Bob nodded slowly, the truth of her words sinking in. "So what do you propose?"

Evelyn's eyes lit up with enthusiasm. "I propose a comprehensive transformation program. Not just changing processes or implementing new technologies, but fundamentally shifting how Maple and Brick operates, innovates, and adapts. It won't be easy, and it won't happen overnight. But if we do this right, in 12 to 18 months, you won't just have solved your current problems -- you'll have built a company that's capable of continually evolving to meet new challenges."

She paused, gauging Bob's reaction. "Of course, this is just an initial assessment. I'd need to do a more thorough analysis, talk to more of your team, and really dig into the data. But I believe Maple and Brick has all the ingredients for a remarkable turnaround. The question is, are you ready for that kind of transformative change?"

Bob took a deep breath, looking out over the factory floor. He thought about the board meeting looming next week, about the challenges they faced, but also about the potential he had seen today -- in Jacob's innovative ideas, in Emily's passion for sustainability, in Joe's wealth of knowledge. He thought about his grandfather, and his ancestors here before that, who had built this company from nothing, always with an eye towards the future.

"Yes," he said finally, his voice firm. "Yes, we're ready. Whatever it takes, we need to do this. For the company, for our people, for the legacy we've built here."

Evelyn smiled, a look of determination in her eyes. "Then let's get to work. We have a lot to do, and not much time. But remember, Bob -- this journey isn't just about saving Maple and Brick. It's about reinventing it for the future. And that future starts now."

As they shook hands, sealing their agreement, Bob felt a surge of energy he hadn't experienced in years. The road ahead would be challenging, but for the first time in a long time, he felt truly hopeful about Maple and Brick's future.

Later that evening, as the factory quieted down for the night, Bob stood alone in his office, looking out over the town of Peterborough. The lights of homes and businesses twinkled in the darkness, each one representing a family, a livelihood, a piece of the community that depended on Maple and Brick.

He thought about the generations of workers who had passed through these factory doors, about the innovations that had been born within these walls. He thought about his great-grandfather's vision, his grandfather's determination, his father's adaptability. And he thought about the responsibility that now rested on his shoulders.

The winds of change were blowing, and they would either tear Maple and Brick apart or propel it into a new era of prosperity. It was up to him to set the sails, to steer the ship through the storm.

As he turned off the lights and prepared to leave, Bob's gaze fell on the framed poem on his desk. The words of his ancestor seemed to take on new meaning now:

"Oh, heir of mine, this tale do keep,

Of those who here did wake and sleep,

Revive their spirit, strong and quick,

In honor of this maple and brick."

Bob smiled to himself. They were about to embark on a journey of revival, of transformation. It wouldn't be easy, but then again, nothing worth doing ever was.

As he locked up the factory and headed to his car, Bob felt a renewed sense of purpose. Tomorrow would bring new challenges, new opportunities, new beginnings. And for the first time in a long time, he was excited to face them head-on.

The winds of change were coming to Maple and Brick. And this time, they were ready to harness their power and soar.

CHAPTER 2 REFLECTION: THE WINDS OF CHANGE

Key Insights:
- ❖ Change is inevitable, but it doesn't have to be disruptive when approached thoughtfully.
- ❖ Recognizing the need for change is the first step towards transformation.

Personal Reflection:

Recall a significant change you've experienced in your life or career. What made it successful or challenging? How did you adapt to this change, and what did you learn from the process?

Application Question:

What changes do you see on the horizon for your life or organization? How can you better prepare yourself and others for these upcoming shifts?

Action Step:

Create a "change readiness" assessment for yourself or your team. List potential changes and rate your preparedness for each.

Quote to Remember:

"The winds of change are not just a force to be weathered – they can be harnessed to propel us forward."

CHAPTER 3: THE RELUCTANT HERO

The early morning light filtered through the windows of Bob Harrington's modest home, casting long shadows across the kitchen table where he sat, nursing a cup of coffee. The house was quiet, his wife Sarah having left for her shift at the local hospital an hour earlier. In the stillness, Bob found himself grappling with the weight of the decisions that lay ahead.

He reached for the well-worn leather journal that had belonged to his great-grandfather, Rhys Morgan. The pages were filled with meticulous notes, innovative sketches, and personal reflections that spanned decades of Maple and Brick's history. Bob had often turned to this journal in times of uncertainty, seeking wisdom from the past to guide him through the present.

As he leafed through the yellowed pages, a loose photograph fluttered to the table. It was a black and white image of Rhys standing proudly in front of the factory, surrounded by a group of workers. Their faces were etched with determination and hope, a stark contrast to the worried expressions Bob had seen on his employees in recent weeks.

"What would you do, Great-Grandpa?" Bob murmured, tracing the outline of Rhys's face with his finger. "How did you find the courage to lead through times of change?"

The sound of his phone ringing jolted Bob from his reverie. It was Evelyn Turner.

"Good morning, Bob," her voice came through, crisp and energetic. "I hope I'm not calling too early. I've been reviewing some of the data from yesterday, and I think we should meet to discuss our next steps. How does 9 AM at the factory sound?"

Bob agreed, feeling a mix of anticipation and dread. As he hung up, his gaze fell on a family photo on the refrigerator – himself, Sarah, and their two children, Emma and Jack. The smiling faces seemed to underscore the stakes of what lay ahead. It wasn't just about saving a company; it was about preserving a legacy, securing a future for his family and the families of everyone who depended on Maple and Brick.

As Bob drove to the factory, the streets of Peterborough were coming to life. He passed by Miller's Hardware, where old Tom Miller was unlocking the front door, just as his father and grandfather had done for generations. The sight of the 'Help Wanted' sign in the window of Johnson's Diner, a local institution, was a stark reminder of the economic challenges facing the town.

Pulling into the factory parking lot, Bob was surprised to see several cars already there, including Evelyn's electric vehicle. As he approached the entrance, he could hear raised voices coming from inside.

Pushing through the doors, Bob found Evelyn engaged in what appeared to be a heated discussion with Joe, the veteran machinist. Laura Mitchell and Jacob stood nearby, looking uncomfortable.

"What's going on here?" Bob asked, his voice cutting through the tension.

Joe turned to him, his face flushed with anger. "Mr. Harrington, this consultant of yours is talking about overhauling our entire production process. She wants to scrap machines that have been the backbone of this factory for decades!"

Evelyn remained calm, her voice level as she addressed Bob. "I was explaining to Joe that some of the older equipment is inefficient and costly to maintain. Upgrading to newer, more flexible systems could significantly improve our productivity and reduce downtime."

Bob felt caught between two worlds – the traditional manufacturing methods that had served them well for so long, and the promise of innovation that Evelyn represented. He could see the merit in both arguments, but the thought of making such drastic changes filled him with unease.

"Let's all take a step back," Bob said, trying to keep his voice steady. "We're not making any decisions without careful consideration. Evelyn, why don't you walk us through your initial findings?"

They moved to the conference room, where Evelyn had set up a presentation. As she began to outline her observations and recommendations, Bob found himself both impressed by her insights and overwhelmed by the scope of changes she was proposing.

"Based on my analysis," Evelyn explained, "Maple and Brick is operating at about 60% efficiency compared to industry standards. By implementing lean manufacturing principles, upgrading key equipment, and retraining staff, we could potentially double our output while reducing costs by 30%."

The numbers were compelling, but Bob could see the skepticism on Joe's face and the worry in Laura's eyes. Jacob, on the other hand, seemed excited by the possibilities.

"That all sounds great on paper," Laura interjected, "but what about our existing contracts? Our customers expect consistency. How do we manage this transition without disrupting our current operations?"

It was a valid concern, one that had been nagging at Bob as well. Evelyn nodded, acknowledging the point.

"That's why I'm proposing a phased approach," she replied. "We'll start with pilot programs in key areas, prove the concept, and then gradually roll out changes across the organization. It's not about dismantling what works, but about enhancing and evolving our capabilities."

As the discussion continued, Bob found his mind wandering. He thought about the generations of workers who had walked these factory floors, about the innovations that had kept Maple and Brick competitive through the years. How many times had the company faced crossroads like this? How many times had a Harrington or a Morgan had to make difficult decisions for the sake of the company's future?

His reverie was interrupted by Joe's gruff voice. "Mr. Harrington, you can't seriously be considering this. We've always done things our way, and it's worked for us. Why fix what ain't broke?"

All eyes turned to Bob, waiting for his response. He felt the weight of their expectations, the weight of history, pressing down on him. In that moment, he realized that this was what leadership truly meant – not having all the answers, but having the courage to seek them out and make tough choices.

Taking a deep breath, Bob addressed the room. "I understand everyone's concerns. Believe me, I share many of them. Change is never easy, especially when we're talking about a company with as rich a history as Maple and Brick. But the reality is, the world is changing around us, and we need to adapt if we want to survive."

He paused, looking each person in the eye before continuing. "That doesn't mean we're going to throw away everything that's made us who we are. Our history, our values, the knowledge and skills of our people – these are our greatest strengths. What Dr. Turner is proposing is a way to build on those strengths, to honor our past by securing our future."

Bob could see a mix of emotions on the faces around him – hope, skepticism, fear, excitement. He knew that his words alone wouldn't be enough to allay all their concerns, but it was a start.

"I'm not asking for blind faith," he continued. "What I am asking for is your trust and your collaboration. We're going to approach this carefully, thoughtfully. We'll pilot new ideas, we'll listen to feedback, and we'll make decisions together. This isn't about imposing change from the top down; it's about working together to shape the future of Maple and Brick."

As the meeting adjourned, Bob could feel the shift in the room's energy. There was still uncertainty, but also a growing sense of possibility. Joe approached him as the others filed out.

"Mr. Harrington," the old machinist said, his voice gruff but tinged with respect, "I can't say I'm entirely convinced about all this. But I've been with this company for forty years, and I've seen a lot of changes. If you think this is the right path, well... I'm willing to give it a shot."

Bob clasped Joe's shoulder, feeling a surge of gratitude. "Thank you, Joe. Your experience and knowledge are going to be crucial as we navigate this. We're going to need your insights every step of the way."

As the day wore on, Bob found himself pulled in a dozen different directions. There were worried employees to reassure, logistical challenges to address, and countless decisions to be made. By the time evening rolled around, he felt drained, both physically and emotionally.

Evelyn found him in his office, staring out the window at the setting sun. "Quite a day, wasn't it?" she said, her voice gentle.

Bob nodded, running a hand through his hair. "I keep asking myself if I'm doing the right thing. What if I'm wrong? What if this whole transformation idea is a mistake?"

Evelyn was quiet for a moment, considering her words carefully. "Bob, do you know what I see when I look at you? I see a leader who cares deeply about his company, his employees, and his community. I see someone who's willing to make hard choices for the greater good, even when it's uncomfortable or scary."

She paused, letting her words sink in. "The fact that you're questioning, that you're not rushing headlong into change without consideration – that's a strength, not a weakness. It means you're approaching this with the care and thoughtfulness it deserves."

Bob turned to face her, feeling a glimmer of the confidence he'd projected earlier in the day. "Thank you, Evelyn. I suppose this is what they call 'the hero's journey,' isn't it? Though I certainly don't feel much like a hero."

Evelyn smiled. "The best heroes are often reluctant ones. They're the ones who step up not because they want glory, but because they know it's necessary. You're not just trying to save a company, Bob. You're fighting for a community, for a way of life. That's pretty heroic in my book."

As Evelyn left, Bob found himself alone with his thoughts once more. He picked up his great-grandfather's journal, flipping through the pages until he came to an entry from the 1930s, during the depths of the Great Depression.

"Times are hard," Rhys had written, "and the path forward is unclear. But I am reminded daily of the resilience of our workers, the strength of our community. We will weather this storm, not by clinging to the past, but by boldly embracing the future. Change is upon us, ready or not. We must find the courage to shape it, rather than be shaped by it."

Bob closed the journal, feeling a renewed sense of purpose. He wasn't just Bob Harrington anymore; he was the latest in a long line of leaders who had guided Maple and Brick through times of change. He was the reluctant hero of this chapter in the company's story.

As he prepared to leave for the night, Bob paused at the factory entrance. The old maple tree stood silhouetted against the twilight sky, its branches reaching upward as if pointing the way forward.

"Alright, old girl," Bob murmured, addressing both the tree and the factory behind it. "Looks like we've got quite a journey ahead of us. But we've weathered storms before, and we'll weather this one too. Together."

With that, Bob stepped out into the cool evening air, ready to face whatever challenges tomorrow might bring. The reluctant hero had taken his first steps on the path of transformation, and there was no turning back now.

CHAPTER 3 REFLECTION: THE RELUCTANT HERO

Key Insights:
- ❖ Leadership often involves stepping up even when you feel unprepared.
- ❖ True leaders find strength in their commitment to others, not in their certainty.

Personal Reflection:

Think of a time when you were thrust into a leadership role unexpectedly. How did you handle it? What did you learn about yourself in that situation?

Application Question:

How can you cultivate the courage to lead in uncertain times, even when you don't feel fully prepared?

Action Step:

Identify one area in your life or work where you've been hesitant to take the lead. Commit to taking one small step towards leadership in this area this week.

Quote to Remember:

"The reluctant hero's journey begins not with confidence, but with the courage to take that first uncertain step."

CHAPTER 4:
A CATALYST ARRIVES

The morning sun had barely crested the horizon when Bob Harrington pulled into the Maple and Brick parking lot. The factory stood silent, awaiting the start of another day. But this day promised to be different from any other in recent memory.

As Bob stepped out of his car, he noticed a sleek, unfamiliar vehicle parked nearby. Standing next to it was a woman he didn't recognize, her posture radiating confidence and purpose. This had to be the expert Evelyn had mentioned – the catalyst who would help jumpstart their transformation.

"Good morning," Bob called out as he approached. "You must be Dr. Alexandra Chen. I'm Bob Harrington."

The woman turned, a warm smile lighting up her face. "Please, call me Alex. It's a pleasure to meet you, Bob. Dr. Turner has told me so much about Maple and Brick. I'm excited to get started."

As they shook hands, Bob couldn't help but feel a mix of anticipation and apprehension. Alex exuded an energy that was both invigorating and slightly intimidating. Her reputation preceded her – a brilliant engineer turned organizational psychologist, known for her innovative approaches to manufacturing transformation.

"Shall we?" Bob gestured towards the factory entrance. As they walked, he couldn't help but notice Alex's keen gaze taking in every detail of their surroundings.

"This building has such character," Alex remarked. "You can feel the history in these walls. How long has Maple and Brick been operating here?"

"Since 1945," Bob replied, a note of pride creeping into his voice. "My great-grandfather started the company right after World War II. It's been in our family ever since."

Alex nodded thoughtfully. "That's quite a legacy. It must add an extra layer of complexity to the transformation process. How are you feeling about all of this, Bob?"

The question caught him off guard. Most consultants he'd met were quick to launch into their own ideas and plans. Alex seemed genuinely interested in his perspective.

"Honestly?" Bob paused, considering his words carefully. "I'm terrified. This company, this building – it's more than just a business. It's my family's legacy, it's the lifeblood of this town. The thought of changing it so fundamentally... it's daunting."

Alex's expression was one of understanding. "That's completely natural, Bob. Change is always scary, especially when there's so much at stake. But from what I've seen and heard, change isn't just an option for Maple and Brick – it's a necessity."

As they entered the factory floor, they were greeted by the familiar hum of machinery and the bustle of the morning shift getting underway. Bob noticed several curious glances directed their way as they made their rounds.

They approached Joe's workstation, where the veteran machinist was already elbow-deep in the inner workings of a temperamental piece of equipment.

"Morning, Mr. Harrington," Joe called out, his voice gruff but not unfriendly. His eyes narrowed slightly as he noticed Alex. "Who's this?"

"Joe, this is Dr. Alexandra Chen. She's here to help us with our... transformation efforts." Bob could hear the hesitation in his own voice.

Joe straightened up, wiping his hands on a rag. "Another consultant, huh? No offense, ma'am, but we've seen plenty of your type come through here. Lots of big ideas, not much practical know-how."

To Bob's surprise, Alex didn't seem offended. Instead, she smiled, stepping closer to examine the machine Joe had been working on. "Is that a Heidelberg GTP? These can be tricky beasts. Mind if I take a look?"

Joe's eyebrows shot up in surprise. "You know your way around machinery?"

"I started my career as an engineer," Alex replied, already peering into the machine's innards. "Spent five years on the factory floor before I moved into organizational psychology. Sometimes I miss getting my hands dirty."

For the next few minutes, Bob watched in amazement as Alex and Joe engaged in a rapid-fire discussion of mechanical troubleshooting. By the end of it, Joe was nodding along, a grudging respect in his eyes.

As they moved on, Bob couldn't help but feel a glimmer of hope. If Alex could win over Joe, even a little, maybe this transformation wasn't impossible after all.

Their next stop was the R&D department, where they found Emily in the midst of what looked like a heated debate with her team.

"I'm telling you, the bonding agent is the key," Emily was saying, her voice passionate. "If we can get that right, the biodegradable polymer could revolutionize our entire product line."

Alex listened intently as Emily explained their current projects and challenges. "Have you considered combining your polymer research with nanotechnology?" she asked. "There's some fascinating work being done in that area that could enhance the material's properties significantly."

Emily's eyes lit up. "I've read about that, but I wasn't sure how to apply it to our specific needs. Do you have any resources you could point me towards?"

As Alex and Emily dove into a discussion of cutting-edge materials science, Bob found himself once again impressed. Alex seemed to have an uncanny ability to speak everyone's language, to find common ground and spark new ideas.

The tour continued, with stops at Jacob's inventory management station, Laura's marketing office, and various production areas. At each stop, Alex listened more than she spoke, asking probing questions and offering insights that seemed to energize and inspire the Maple and Brick team.

By lunchtime, there was a palpable buzz in the air. Bob could see small groups of employees huddled in discussion, their faces animated in a way he hadn't seen in months.

As they settled into Bob's office for a debrief, Alex's expression was thoughtful. "You have an incredible team here, Bob. There's so much potential, so much passion. But there's also a lot of fear and resistance to change."

Bob nodded, feeling a weight settle on his shoulders. "I know. We've been doing things the same way for so long. How do we overcome that inertia?"

Alex leaned forward, her eyes intense. "By tapping into the very thing that makes Maple and Brick special – its history, its community, its people. We're not going to impose change from the outside. We're going to catalyze it from within."

She pulled out a notebook, quickly sketching out a diagram. "I'm proposing a three-pronged approach. First, we'll create cross-functional innovation teams, bringing together people from different departments to tackle specific challenges. This will break down silos and foster collaboration."

Bob nodded, intrigued. "And the other two prongs?"

"Second, we'll implement a mentorship program, pairing experienced employees like Joe with younger team members. This will ensure that valuable institutional knowledge isn't lost, while also exposing long-time employees to fresh perspectives."

"Finally," Alex continued, her voice filled with excitement, "we're going to launch what I call the 'Heritage Innovation Initiative.' We'll challenge teams to find ways to honor Maple and Brick's rich history while pushing the boundaries of innovation. This could involve reimagining traditional products with cutting-edge materials, or finding modern applications for historical patents and techniques."

As Alex outlined her plan in more detail, Bob felt a spark of excitement ignite within him. This wasn't about throwing away everything they'd built. It was about building on their strengths, about honoring their past while embracing the future.

"What do you think, Bob?" Alex asked, finally pausing for breath. "I know it's a lot to take in."

Bob was quiet for a moment, his mind racing with possibilities. He thought about Joe's grudging respect for Alex, about the light in Emily's eyes as they discussed new technologies. He thought about the generations of workers who had passed through these halls, each leaving their mark on Maple and Brick's legacy.

Finally, he spoke. "I think... I think this could work. It won't be easy, but I believe in our people. If we can channel their passion and expertise in the right direction, there's no limit to what we can achieve."

Alex's smile was radiant. "That's exactly the attitude we need, Bob. You're not just the leader of this company – you're the bridge between its past and its future. Your belief in your team, your commitment to this community – that's going to be the fuel that drives this transformation."

As they stood to leave, Bob felt a renewed sense of purpose. The day had started with apprehension, but it was ending with hope. Alex wasn't just a consultant – she was truly a catalyst, igniting the spark of change that had been dormant within Maple and Brick.

Walking back onto the factory floor, Bob could feel the energy in the air. The winds of change were no longer just a distant breeze – they were gathering force, ready to sweep through Maple and Brick. And for the first time in a long time, Bob felt ready to spread his sails and harness their power.

The transformation of Maple and Brick was no longer just a vague concept. With Alex's arrival, it had become a tangible reality, full of challenges and opportunities. As the afternoon sun streamed through the factory windows, Bob Harrington stood tall, ready to lead his company into a new era.

The catalyst had arrived, and there was no turning back now.

CHAPTER 4 REFLECTION: A CATALYST ARRIVES

Key Insights:
- ❖ Sometimes, an external perspective is necessary to unlock internal potential.
- ❖ Embracing new ideas and viewpoints can catalyze transformative change.

Personal Reflection:

Recall a time when an outsider's perspective significantly changed your approach to a problem or situation. How did this new viewpoint impact your thinking and actions?

Application Question:

Who could you invite into your circle to provide a fresh perspective on your current challenges?

Action Step:

Reach out to someone outside your usual network and ask for their input on a problem you're currently facing.

Quote to Remember:

"The spark of transformation often comes from the most unexpected sources."

CHAPTER 5: RESISTANCE AND DOUBT

The excitement that had filled Maple and Brick following Alex's arrival began to wane as the reality of change set in. Two weeks into the transformation process, Bob Harrington found himself navigating a minefield of resistance and doubt that seemed to grow with each passing day.

The morning started with a tense meeting in the conference room. Bob sat at the head of the table, flanked by Alex and Evelyn, facing a group of department heads whose expressions ranged from skeptical to openly hostile.

Laura Mitchell, head of sales, was the first to speak up. "Bob, I understand the need for change, but this 'Heritage Innovation Initiative' is causing havoc with our existing clients. They're worried about consistency and quality. We've already lost two small contracts, and Aerodyne is threatening to take their business elsewhere if we can't guarantee that our 'innovations' won't affect their supply chain."

Bob felt a knot form in his stomach. Losing Aerodyne would be a devastating blow. Before he could respond, Joe, the veteran machinist, chimed in.

"And these 'cross-functional teams' are a mess," Joe grumbled. "We've got marketing people trying to tell us how to run our machines, and R&D folks who've never seen a production line thinking they can revolutionize our processes overnight. It's chaos out there."

Emily, usually the most enthusiastic about change, looked uncomfortable. "I hate to add to the negativity, but we're facing some challenges in R&D too. The new biodegradable polymer isn't performing as well as we'd hoped in stress tests. We might need to go back to the drawing board, which could set us back months."

Bob glanced at Alex, hoping for support. She met his gaze steadily, her expression calm but concerned.

"I understand everyone's frustrations," Alex began, her voice level. "Change is never easy, and what we're attempting here is a significant transformation. It's normal to encounter obstacles and setbacks along the way."

"Normal?" Laura interjected. "We're talking about the survival of this company. These aren't just 'obstacles' – they're existential threats."

Bob took a deep breath, trying to project a confidence he didn't entirely feel. "I hear all of your concerns, and they're valid. But let's remember why we started down this path. Maple and Brick was facing decline. We needed to change to survive. Yes, it's difficult, and yes, there are risks. But the biggest risk of all would be to do nothing."

The room fell silent for a moment, the weight of Bob's words sinking in. Finally, Jacob, the young shipping supervisor, spoke up.

"Mr. Harrington is right," he said, his voice slightly shaky but gaining strength. "I know the new inventory system has been causing headaches, but I can already see improvements in our efficiency. We just need time to work out the kinks."

Bob felt a surge of gratitude towards Jacob. It wasn't much, but it was a start. "Thank you, Jacob. Now, let's address these issues one by one. Laura, can you set up a meeting with Aerodyne? I want to walk them through our plans personally, show them how our innovations will ultimately benefit them."

Laura nodded, still looking skeptical but slightly mollified.

"Joe," Bob continued, "I want you to take the lead on integrating the cross-functional teams in production. Your experience is invaluable –

help the newer team members understand our processes, and be open to their fresh perspectives."

Joe grumbled but didn't object outright.

"Emily, don't lose heart. Setbacks in R&D are part of the process. Let's allocate some additional resources to the polymer project. And maybe we can get some outside expertise to consult on the stress test issues."

As the meeting adjourned, Bob felt drained. The road ahead seemed longer and more treacherous than ever. Alex lingered behind as the others filed out.

"That was a tough crowd," she said, her tone sympathetic but not pitying. "But you handled it well, Bob. Leadership isn't about having all the answers – it's about asking the right questions and guiding your team towards solutions."

Bob appreciated her words, but doubt gnawed at him. "I'm starting to wonder if I'm the right person to lead this transformation, Alex. Maybe the board should bring in someone with more experience in change management."

Alex's expression turned serious. "Bob, do you know why I agreed to take on this project? It wasn't just because of Maple and Brick's potential for innovation. It was because of you."

Bob looked at her, surprised. "Me?"

"Yes, you," Alex continued. "I've worked with many CEOs, and most of them see their companies as nothing more than balance sheets and profit margins. But you... you understand that Maple and Brick is more than just a business. It's a community, a legacy. That kind of leadership can't be imported or manufactured. It's ingrained in the very DNA of this company through you."

Her words buoyed Bob's spirits, but the doubt wasn't entirely gone. As they left the conference room, the sounds of the factory floor reached them – the hum of machinery intermingled with voices raised in what sounded like an argument.

They rounded the corner to find a small crowd gathered around Joe and one of the younger engineers from the cross-functional team. The two men were engaged in a heated debate about the best way to optimize the production line for a new product.

"Listen, kid," Joe was saying, his face red with frustration, "I've been running these machines since before you were born. You can't just come in here with your fancy algorithms and expect to revolutionize everything overnight!"

The young engineer, whose name tag read 'Mike,' stood his ground. "I'm not trying to revolutionize everything, Joe. I'm just saying that if we adjust the feed rate and recalibrate the pressure sensors, we could increase output by 15% without sacrificing quality."

Bob was about to intervene when Alex put a hand on his arm, silently signaling him to wait. She stepped forward, addressing both men.

"Gentlemen," she said, her voice cutting through the tension, "it seems to me you're both partially right. Joe, your experience with these machines is invaluable. You understand their quirks and capabilities in a way that no algorithm can replicate. And Mike, your fresh perspective and knowledge of new technologies offer opportunities for improvement that we'd be foolish to ignore."

She paused, looking between the two men. "What if, instead of arguing, you worked together to find a solution that incorporates both of your insights? Joe, could you show Mike how you've optimized the machines over the years? And Mike, could you explain your proposed changes in more detail, so Joe can see how they might enhance his existing methods?"

The two men looked at each other, the anger in their expressions slowly giving way to grudging respect. Joe nodded slowly. "I suppose I could do that. Come on, kid. Let me show you how this old girl really works."

As Joe led Mike towards the production line, the crowd dispersed, returning to their tasks. Bob turned to Alex, impressed. "That was skillfully handled. How did you know that would work?"

Alex smiled. "Conflict like that is often a sign that we're on the verge of a breakthrough. When old ways and new ideas collide, it can be messy. But if we can channel that energy constructively, that's where real innovation happens."

As they continued their walk through the factory, Bob noticed other small signs of the transformation in progress. In one corner, Emily was deep in conversation with a supplier, discussing the possibility of sourcing more sustainable materials. Near the shipping area, Jacob was demonstrating the new inventory system to a group of workers, their initial skepticism giving way to cautious interest as they saw the system in action.

But for every positive sign, there seemed to be a counterbalance of resistance. Bob overheard snippets of conversation that made his heart sink:

"If they think I'm going to learn a whole new system at my age, they've got another thing coming..."

"I heard they're planning layoffs once all these new processes are in place..."

"My cousin works at that new tech startup in Manchester. Says they're always hiring..."

The doubts that Bob had momentarily shaken off in the conference room came flooding back. Were they moving too fast? Was he pushing his people too hard? What if this transformation ended up destroying the very thing he was trying to save?

As if reading his thoughts, Alex spoke up. "You're wondering if you're doing the right thing, aren't you?"

Bob nodded, not trusting himself to speak.

"Let me tell you something I've learned in my years of doing this work," Alex continued. "Doubt is not the enemy of transformation. In fact, it's an essential part of the process. It forces us to question our assumptions, to refine our approaches, to make sure we're on the right path."

They paused near the old maple tree that stood outside the factory entrance. Alex gestured towards it. "Look at this tree. It's been here for generations, right? But it didn't survive this long by remaining rigid and unchanging. Every year, it sheds its leaves, endures the winter, and grows anew in the spring. That process of renewal isn't always pretty or comfortable, but it's necessary for survival and growth."

Bob considered her words, finding comfort in the analogy. "So you're saying this resistance, these setbacks – they're all part of our renewal process?"

"Exactly," Alex nodded. "The key is to not let the doubt paralyze you, but to let it inform and guide you. Use it to refine your approach, to address valid concerns, to bring your team along with you on this journey."

As they stood there, the factory humming behind them and the old maple tree standing tall before them, Bob felt a renewed sense of purpose. Yes, the path ahead was challenging. Yes, there would be resistance and setbacks. But with each obstacle overcome, with each doubt addressed, they were moving closer to becoming the company they needed to be.

"Thank you, Alex," Bob said finally. "I needed that perspective. Now, let's get back in there and face these challenges head-on."

As they turned to re-enter the factory, Bob caught sight of a small green shoot emerging from a crack in the pavement near the maple tree's roots. It was a tiny thing, barely noticeable, but to Bob, it felt like a sign. Even in the midst of concrete and asphalt, life found a way to push through, to grow, to transform.

The rest of the day was a whirlwind of meetings, problem-solving sessions, and one-on-one conversations with concerned employees. Bob found himself drawing on reserves of patience and empathy he didn't know he possessed. With each interaction, he tried to channel Alex's wisdom – acknowledging doubts and fears while gently but firmly steering the conversation towards solutions and possibilities.

By the time evening fell, Bob was exhausted but oddly invigorated. The challenges they faced were still immense, but somehow, they felt more manageable. As he prepared to leave for the night, he paused in front of the framed poem on his office wall, the one written by his great-great grandmother Sarah Morgan.

"Oh, heir of mine, this tale do keep,

Of those who here did wake and sleep,

Revive their spirit, strong and quick,

In honor of this maple and brick."

The words took on new meaning now. Bob realized that he wasn't just trying to save a company – he was reviving a spirit, a legacy of innovation and perseverance that had seen Maple and Brick through countless challenges over the decades.

As he switched off the lights and stepped out into the cool evening air, Bob felt a sense of calm determination settle over him. The doubts and resistance they faced were not obstacles to be overcome, but integral parts of their transformation journey. Each challenge was an opportunity to grow stronger, to become more resilient, to honor the legacy of Maple and Brick while forging a new path forward.

The old maple tree stood silhouetted against the twilight sky, its branches reaching upward as if pointing the way forward. Bob smiled to himself, feeling a kinship with the ancient tree. Like Maple and Brick, it had weathered countless storms, shed old layers, and continually renewed itself.

Tomorrow would bring new challenges, new doubts, and new resistance. But it would also bring new opportunities, new ideas, and new growth. And Bob Harrington was ready to face it all, rooted in the rich soil of Maple and Brick's history while reaching towards a future full of possibility.

CHAPTER 5 REFLECTION: RESISTANCE AND DOUBT

Key Insights:
- ❖ Resistance is a natural part of the change process and can be a sign of progress.
- ❖ Doubt can be transformed into a constructive force for improvement.

Personal Reflection:

Consider a time when you faced significant resistance to a new idea or change you proposed. How did you handle it? What did this experience teach you about perseverance and adaptation?

Application Question:

How can you reframe resistance and doubt as opportunities for growth and refinement in your current projects or goals?

Action Step:

Identify the biggest source of resistance in your current endeavors. Develop a strategy to address it constructively, focusing on understanding its root causes.

Quote to Remember:

"In the face of doubt, we find our true strength; in overcoming resistance, we forge our path forward."

CHAPTER 6:
THE FIRST STEPS

The early morning mist clung to the ground as Bob Harrington pulled into the Maple and Brick parking lot. The factory loomed before him, its brick facade tinged orange by the rising sun. Today marked the official launch of their transformation initiatives, and Bob felt a mix of excitement and trepidation churning in his stomach.

As he approached the entrance, he noticed Alex Chen already there, engaged in conversation with Joe and Jacob. The unlikely trio seemed deep in discussion, with Joe gesticulating animatedly while Jacob nodded, his eyes bright with interest.

"Good morning," Bob called out as he neared the group. "You're all here early."

Alex turned, a smile lighting up her face. "Bob! We were just discussing the first steps of our cross-functional team initiative. Joe here has some fascinating insights on how we can merge traditional techniques with new technologies."

Joe looked slightly embarrassed but pleased. "Well, I wouldn't say fascinating. Just some ideas I've been kicking around. Figured if we're gonna do this thing, might as well do it right."

Bob felt a surge of hope. If Joe, their most vocal skeptic, was already engaging with the process, maybe they were on the right track after all.

As they entered the factory, Bob was struck by the buzz of activity. Usually, the early morning hours were quiet, with just the hum of machinery as the first shift got underway. Today, however, there was an energy in the air, a sense of anticipation.

Emily rushed up to them, her lab coat fluttering behind her. "Mr. Harrington, Dr. Chen, you won't believe what we've discovered! Remember those stress test issues we were having with the biodegradable polymer? Well, we had a breakthrough last night. If we incorporate nanoparticles into the polymer matrix, we can significantly enhance its mechanical properties without compromising its biodegradability!"

Alex's eyes lit up. "That's fantastic, Emily! Have you considered the scalability of this approach? And what about potential applications beyond your current product line?"

As Emily and Alex dove into a technical discussion, Bob marveled at the transformation he was witnessing. Just days ago, the mood had been tense, filled with doubt and resistance. Now, there was a palpable sense of possibility in the air.

The day unfolded in a whirlwind of activity. Bob found himself moving from one area of the factory to another, observing and participating in the various initiatives they had put in place.

In the production area, the first cross-functional team was already hard at work. Joe stood at a whiteboard, sketching out the current production flow while Mike, the young engineer, overlaid it with a digital projection of proposed optimizations. Other team members, drawn from various departments, chimed in with questions and suggestions.

"See here," Joe was saying, pointing to a particular stage in the process. "This is where we've always had a bottleneck. But if we combine Mike's algorithm with some good old-fashioned mechanical tweaks, I think we can smooth it out."

Mike nodded enthusiastically. "Exactly! And by integrating real-time data from the sensors we installed last week, we can make adjustments on the fly, further optimizing the process."

Bob watched in amazement as ideas flowed back and forth, with team members building on each other's suggestions. This was exactly what they had hoped for when they conceived the cross-functional teams

– a synergy of experience and innovation, of old wisdom and new techniques.

In another corner of the factory, the Heritage Innovation Initiative was taking shape. Laura from marketing was leading a brainstorming session, surrounded by an eclectic group that included long-time employees, new hires, and even a local historian they had invited to consult.

"Alright, folks," Laura was saying, her earlier skepticism replaced by focused energy. "We're not just talking about updating our product line. We're looking to tap into Maple and Brick's rich history to create something truly unique. What stories can we tell through our products? How can we honor our heritage while pushing the boundaries of innovation?"

Ideas began to flow: A line of high-tech outdoor gear inspired by the rugged spirit of New Hampshire's early settlers. Smart home devices housed in casings that echoed the aesthetic of vintage radios. Biodegradable packaging that incorporated designs from the company's early textile patterns.

As Bob listened, he felt a swell of pride. This was more than just a marketing exercise – it was a rediscovery of Maple and Brick's identity, a bridge between past and future.

The day wasn't without its challenges, of course. In the shipping department, Jacob was grappling with unexpected glitches in the new inventory management system. A small crowd had gathered, tension rising as delays began to pile up.

"I don't understand," Jacob muttered, frustration evident in his voice as he stared at the computer screen. "It was working fine yesterday."

Bob was about to step in when he saw Alex approaching, a calm presence amidst the growing chaos.

"Jacob," she said softly, "walk me through what you're seeing. Sometimes, explaining a problem out loud can help us see it in a new light."

As Jacob began to describe the issue, Bob saw the young man's shoulders relax slightly. Alex listened intently, asking clarifying questions and offering gentle suggestions. Gradually, other team members began to chime in, offering their own observations and ideas.

Within an hour, they had not only identified the root of the problem – a minor but crucial error in how the system was interpreting data from one of the production lines – but had also devised a temporary workaround and a plan for a permanent fix.

"You see," Alex said to the group as they implemented the solution, "this is exactly why we're going through this transformation. It's not just about new systems or processes. It's about developing our problem-solving muscles, about learning to collaborate and innovate in real-time."

As the day wore on, Bob found himself constantly amazed by the resilience and creativity of his team. Yes, there were setbacks and moments of frustration. But for every obstacle they encountered, he saw people coming together to find solutions, often in ways that surprised him.

In the R&D lab, Emily and her team were already running simulations on their nanoparticle-enhanced polymer, excitedly discussing potential applications that went far beyond their original scope. In the maintenance department, Joe was working side by side with the IT team, his decades of mechanical knowledge proving invaluable as they integrated new sensors and monitoring systems into the older machinery.

Even Laura, who had been one of the most vocal skeptics, seemed to have found her stride. Bob overheard her on the phone with a client, enthusiastically describing how Maple and Brick's new initiatives would ultimately lead to better products and more reliable service.

As the day drew to a close, Bob gathered everyone in the main assembly area for a brief address. Looking out over the sea of faces – some tired, some excited, all attentive – he felt a surge of emotion.

"First of all," he began, his voice carrying across the suddenly quiet factory floor, "I want to thank each and every one of you for your hard work and dedication today. What I've seen – what we've all seen – is nothing short of remarkable."

He paused, looking from face to face, acknowledging each person's contribution with a nod or a smile.

"I know these changes haven't been easy. I know there have been moments of doubt, moments of frustration. But today, you've all shown what Maple and Brick is truly capable of. You've demonstrated the innovative spirit, the resilience, and the teamwork that have been the hallmarks of this company for generations."

Bob gestured around the factory, to the machines both old and new, to the whiteboards covered in fresh ideas, to the prototypes and samples of new products.

"What we're doing here isn't just about saving a company. It's about honoring our past by securing our future. It's about taking the best of what Maple and Brick has always been and combining it with new ideas, new technologies, new ways of thinking."

He could see heads nodding, could feel the energy in the room building.

"Today was just the first step on a long journey. There will be more challenges ahead, more obstacles to overcome. But after what I've seen today, I have no doubt that we're on the right path. Together, we're not just transforming Maple and Brick – we're redefining what's possible in American manufacturing."

As a cheer went up from the assembled employees, Bob felt a hand on his shoulder. He turned to see Alex, her eyes shining with pride and excitement.

"Well done, Bob," she said softly. "You're not just leading a transformation – you're inspiring a movement."

Later that evening, as the factory quieted and the last employees trickled out, Bob found himself once again standing beneath the old maple tree. The day's last light filtered through its leaves, casting dappled shadows on the ground.

Alex joined him, her presence a quiet comfort after the intensity of the day.

"You know," Bob said, his voice thoughtful, "my great-grandfather used to say that this tree was the heart of Maple and Brick. That as long as it stood strong, so would we."

Alex nodded, her gaze traveling up the gnarled trunk to the spreading canopy above. "Trees are remarkable things. They grow slowly, almost imperceptibly, but they're constantly adapting to their environment. They bend with the wind, their roots seek out new sources of nourishment, their leaves turn to catch the sun."

She turned to Bob, her expression serious but kind. "That's what you're doing with Maple and Brick, Bob. You're helping it adapt, helping it grow. It may not always be visible day-to-day, but the changes you're making now will shape the company for generations to come."

Bob felt the weight of that responsibility, but also the exhilaration of possibility. "It's not just me," he said. "It's all of us. Every person in that factory, from Joe with his decades of experience to our newest intern – they're all part of this growth."

As they stood there in the gathering twilight, Bob reflected on the day's events. Yes, it had been challenging. Yes, there would be more obstacles ahead. But they had taken their first steps on this journey of transformation, and already he could see the impact.

He thought of Emily's excitement over the new polymer, of Joe and Mike finding common ground in their quest to optimize the production line. He thought of Laura's newfound enthusiasm for the Heritage Innovation Initiative, and Jacob's perseverance in the face of technical difficulties.

These were more than just isolated incidents. They were the first shoots of a new Maple and Brick, one that honored its roots while reaching for new heights.

As Bob and Alex turned to leave, a gentle breeze rustled through the maple's leaves. To Bob, it sounded almost like applause – nature's own acknowledgment of their efforts.

The first steps had been taken. The path ahead was long and uncertain, but they were on their way. And with each challenge overcome, with each innovation birthed, with each collaboration forged, Maple and Brick was growing stronger, more resilient, more ready to face the future.

As they walked back towards the factory, Bob felt a renewed sense of purpose. Tomorrow would bring new challenges, new opportunities for growth. But now, he knew they were ready to face them – not as individuals, but as a team, as a community, as Maple and Brick reborn.

The transformation had begun, and there was no turning back. The winds of change were no longer just a distant breeze – they were a force propelling Maple and Brick into a new era of innovation and possibility. On his way home, Bob drove past the barn that housed the Peterborough Players theatre. The thought of world-class performance taking place in this rustic setting never failed to fill him with pride for this town's rich cultural heritage.

CHAPTER 6 REFLECTION: THE FIRST STEPS

Key Insights:
- ❖ The initial steps in any transformation are often the most challenging but crucial for building momentum.
- ❖ Small wins can lay the foundation for larger successes.

Personal Reflection:

Think about a project or goal where you initially struggled to make progress. What finally helped you gain momentum? How did those first steps feel, and what did they lead to?

Application Question:

What small, achievable step can you take today to move closer to a significant goal or change you've been contemplating?

Action Step:

Identify three "quick wins" you can accomplish in the next week that will build momentum towards your larger objectives.

Quote to Remember:

"Every journey of transformation begins with a single step, no matter how small or uncertain it may seem."

CHAPTER 7: UNEARTHING THE PAST

The soft glow of dawn was just beginning to illuminate the sky as Bob Harrington made his way through the quiet streets of Peterborough. The town was still asleep, but Bob's mind was already racing with the day ahead. It had been three weeks since they'd launched their transformation initiatives, and while progress was being made, he couldn't shake the feeling that something was missing.

As he approached the factory, Bob noticed a figure standing beneath the old maple tree. It was Joe, the veteran machinist, looking up at the branches with a thoughtful expression.

"Morning, Joe," Bob called out as he drew near. "You're here early."

Joe turned, a wry smile on his weathered face. "Morning, Mr. Harrington. Just thinking about old times. This tree's seen a lot of changes over the years."

Bob nodded, sensing an opportunity. "I bet you have too. You've been with Maple and Brick longer than anyone else here."

"Forty-three years next month," Joe said, a note of pride in his voice. "Started as an apprentice right out of high school. Back then, we were still doing a lot of textile work. The shift to plastics and electronics… that was a big change."

Bob's interest was piqued. "How did the company handle that transition?"

Joe's brow furrowed as he recalled. "It wasn't easy. Lot of folks were resistant at first. But your grandfather, he had a way of bringing people along. He'd say, 'We're not leaving our past behind, we're building on it.' Started a program to retrain the textile workers for the new production lines. Even kept some of the old looms running for specialty orders."

As Joe continued to reminisce, Bob felt a spark of inspiration. Here was a living connection to Maple and Brick's history, a repository of knowledge that could prove invaluable to their current transformation efforts.

Their conversation was interrupted by the arrival of Alex, who approached with a curious expression. "Good morning, gentlemen. What's got you two out here so early?"

Bob quickly filled her in on their discussion. Alex's eyes lit up with interest. "Joe, your experiences could be incredibly valuable to our Heritage Innovation Initiative. Would you be willing to share some of your stories with the team?"

Joe looked surprised but pleased. "Well, I suppose I could. Never thought anyone would be interested in an old timer's ramblings."

As they made their way into the factory, Bob's mind was racing with possibilities. If Joe's memories held such insights, what other pieces of Maple and Brick's history might be waiting to be rediscovered?

The day unfolded with a new energy. Word of Joe's impromptu history lesson spread quickly, and soon other long-time employees were coming forward with their own stories and memories.

In the conference room, Laura had set up a makeshift "memory wall," covered with old photographs, newspaper clippings, and handwritten notes. Employees gathered around, pointing out familiar faces and places, sharing anecdotes that spanned decades.

"Look at this," Emily exclaimed, holding up a faded photograph. "It's the original R&D lab. They were working on synthetic fibers back in the 1950s. We thought we were the first to explore sustainable materials, but it looks like Maple and Brick has always been at the forefront of innovation."

Bob watched as connections were made and ideas began to flow. The Heritage Innovation Initiative was taking on a new dimension, grounded in the rich soil of Maple and Brick's history.

As the afternoon wore on, Bob found himself drawn to his office. There was something nagging at the back of his mind, a half-remembered conversation with his father years ago. He began rifling through the old filing cabinets, searching for something he wasn't even sure existed.

After an hour of fruitless searching, Bob was about to give up when his hand brushed against a small, hidden latch in the back of the bottom drawer. With a click, a secret compartment sprang open, revealing a dusty leather-bound journal and a folder filled with what looked like old blueprints.

Heart racing, Bob carefully extracted the items and laid them on his desk. The journal bore the name "Rhys Morgan" – his great-grandfather, the man who had truly put Maple and Brick on the map.

As Bob began to leaf through the pages, he felt as if he was stepping back in time. Rhys's neat handwriting filled page after page with observations, ideas, and sketches. It was more than just a record of business transactions; it was a window into the mind of an innovator.

One entry in particular caught Bob's eye:

"May 15, 1932 – These are dark times for Maple and Brick, and for the nation as a whole. The Great Depression has hit us hard, and many are calling for us to scale back, to play it safe. But I cannot shake the feeling that now, more than ever, is the time for bold action. We must innovate not in spite of the challenges we face, but because of them. I have an idea for a new type of synthetic fiber, one that could revolutionize our product line and possibly save the company. It's risky, but as I told Sarah last night, 'The greatest risk is in standing still while the world moves forward.'"

Bob felt a chill run down his spine. His great-grandfather's words could have been written about their current situation. The parallels were uncanny.

He was so engrossed in the journal that he didn't hear Alex enter the office. "Bob? What have you got there?"

Looking up, Bob saw Alex's curious expression. "I think I've just found a piece of Maple and Brick's soul," he said, his voice filled with awe.

Over the next hour, Bob and Alex pored over the journal and blueprints. They discovered detailed plans for innovations that were decades ahead of their time, strategies for navigating economic downturns, and philosophical musings on the nature of business and community.

"This is incredible," Alex breathed, her eyes shining with excitement. "Bob, do you realize what this means? You're not just the current CEO of Maple and Brick – you're the heir to a legacy of innovation and resilience."

Bob nodded, feeling a mix of pride and responsibility wash over him. "We need to share this with the team," he said. "This isn't just about honoring our past; it's about reconnecting with the innovative spirit that's always been at the heart of Maple and Brick."

As they made their way back to the factory floor, Bob's mind was racing with possibilities. How could they integrate these historical insights into their current initiatives? How could they use the wisdom of the past to inform their path forward?

They found the team gathered around the memory wall, still buzzing with energy from the day's discoveries. Bob cleared his throat, drawing everyone's attention.

"Everyone, I have something I need to share with you," he began, holding up the journal and blueprints. "These belonged to my great-grandfather, Rhys Morgan. They're not just historical artifacts – they're a roadmap for innovation, a testament to the resilience and creativity that have always been at the heart of Maple and Brick."

As Bob began to read excerpts from the journal, a hush fell over the room. Employees listened intently, their expressions a mix of wonder and dawning understanding.

Emily was the first to speak up. "Mr. Harrington, this is amazing. Rhys's ideas about sustainable materials – they're not that different from what we're working on now. We're not just innovating; we're continuing a legacy!"

Joe nodded, a glimmer of pride in his eyes. "I always knew there was something special about this place. It's not just a factory – it's a… a crucible for ideas."

As the team began to discuss how they could incorporate these historical insights into their current projects, Bob felt a surge of emotion. This wasn't just about saving a company anymore. It was about honoring a legacy, about reconnecting with the innovative spirit that had seen Maple and Brick through countless challenges over the decades.

Alex caught his eye, a knowing smile on her face. "You see, Bob? The answers you've been looking for – they've been here all along. Sometimes, to move forward, we need to look back."

As the day drew to a close, Bob found himself once again standing beneath the old maple tree. The setting sun painted the sky in hues of orange and pink, casting a warm glow over the factory.

He opened his Grandfather's journal, turning to the final entry:

"December 31, 1965 – As I prepare to hand over the reins of Maple and Brick to the next generation, I find myself reflecting on the journey that has brought us here. We have weathered storms, embraced change, and always strived to push the boundaries of what's possible. But our greatest strength has never been in our machines or our products. It has been in our people – in their creativity, their resilience, their unwavering commitment to this company and this community. To those who will lead Maple and Brick into the future: Never forget where you came from, but never be afraid to reimagine where you might go. The spirit of innovation that has brought us this far will carry you forward, as long as you have the courage to nurture it."

Bob closed the journal, feeling a renewed sense of purpose. They had unearthed more than just old documents and memories today. They had rediscovered the very essence of Maple and Brick – an unbroken thread of innovation and resilience that stretched back generations.

As he turned to head home, Bob's gaze fell on the factory. In the fading light, he could almost see the ghosts of the past – the textile workers, the wartime production lines, the countless men and women who had poured their hearts and souls into this place. But he could also see the future – the cross-functional teams, the sustainable materials, the fusion of tradition and cutting-edge technology.

Maple and Brick's transformation was no longer just about adapting to survive. It was about reclaiming their heritage as innovators, as problem-solvers, as a force for positive change in their industry and their community.

With the journal tucked safely under his arm, Bob walked towards his car, his step light despite the long day. Tomorrow would bring new challenges, new opportunities to apply the wisdom of the past to the problems of the present. But now, armed with the knowledge of where they had come from, Bob felt more confident than ever about where they were going.

The winds of change were still blowing, but now they carried with them the whispers of the past – a chorus of voices urging them forward, reminding them of the resilience and creativity that had always been the true strength of Maple and Brick.

CHAPTER 7 REFLECTION: UNEARTHING THE PAST

Key Insights:
- ❖ The past holds valuable lessons that can guide future innovation.
- ❖ Understanding our history can provide a blueprint for addressing modern challenges.

Personal Reflection:
Reflect on a past experience or lesson that has significantly shaped your current approach to work or life. How has this historical knowledge informed your decision-making?

Application Question:
How can you more effectively draw on the wisdom of the past to address your current challenges and fuel innovation?

Action Step:
Research the history of your organization or field. Identify one forgotten practice or idea that could be relevant to a current challenge you're facing.

Quote to Remember:
"Our past is not just a legacy to be preserved, but a wellspring of wisdom to be tapped for future growth."

CHAPTER 8:
ALLIES AND ADVERSARIES

The morning sun had barely crested the horizon when Bob Harrington arrived at Maple and Brick. The factory stood silent, awaiting the start of another day that promised both challenges and opportunities. As Bob made his way to the entrance, he noticed a sleek black car pulling into the parking lot. His heart sank as he recognized the vehicle – it belonged to Richard Hawthorne, the chairman of the board.

Richard stepped out of the car, his crisp suit and stern expression a stark contrast to the casual attire of the early-shift workers trickling in. "Bob," he called out, his voice carrying across the parking lot. "We need to talk."

Bob steeled himself as he approached. Richard's unexpected visits rarely boded well. "Good morning, Richard. I wasn't expecting you today."

"Clearly," Richard replied, his tone clipped. "I've been hearing some... concerning reports about the changes you're implementing here. The board is worried, Bob. We're not seeing the immediate results we were hoping for."

Before Bob could respond, they were interrupted by the arrival of Alex Chen. She approached with a confident stride, seemingly unfazed by Richard's imposing presence.

"Mr. Hawthorne," she said, extending her hand. "I'm Dr. Alexandra Chen. I've been working with Bob on Maple and Brick's transformation strategy."

Richard shook her hand briefly, his expression guarded. "Ah yes, the consultant. Perhaps you can explain to me why we're pouring resources into what seems to be a wild goose chase of 'innovation' when our core business is suffering?"

Alex met his gaze steadily. "Mr. Hawthorne, I understand your concerns. Transformation is never a linear process. But if you have a moment, I'd like to show you exactly what we've been working on. I think you'll find that we're not chasing geese, but rather cultivating golden eggs."

Richard raised an eyebrow, a mix of skepticism and curiosity in his eyes. "Very well. Lead the way."

As they entered the factory, Bob couldn't help but feel a sense of trepidation. Richard's presence added a new layer of pressure to their already challenging journey. But as they moved through the facility, he began to see their progress through fresh eyes.

In the R&D lab, Emily was already hard at work with her team. She looked up as they entered, her face lighting up with excitement. "Mr. Harrington! Dr. Chen! You're just in time. We've made a breakthrough with the nanoparticle-enhanced polymer."

Richard looked intrigued despite himself. "Nanoparticle-enhanced polymer?"

Emily nodded enthusiastically. "Yes, sir. By incorporating nanoparticles into our biodegradable polymer matrix, we've created a material that's not only eco-friendly but also stronger and more versatile than anything we've produced before. We're looking at potential applications in everything from medical devices to aerospace components."

As Emily launched into a more detailed explanation, complete with samples and test results, Bob watched Richard's expression change from skepticism to genuine interest.

"And how soon could this be market-ready?" Richard asked.

Emily glanced at Bob before answering. "With proper funding and support, we could have a prototype ready for testing within three months, and full-scale production within a year."

Richard nodded thoughtfully. "Impressive. Very impressive indeed."

Their next stop was the production floor, where Joe and Mike were overseeing the implementation of their optimized production line. The space hummed with energy, a seamless blend of experienced workers and cutting-edge technology.

"Production efficiency is up 22% since we implemented the new system," Mike reported, his eyes shining with pride. "And that's just the beginning. As we fine-tune the AI-driven predictive maintenance protocols, we're expecting to see even greater improvements in uptime and output quality."

Joe chimed in, his gruff voice tinged with excitement. "And the best part is, we're not just working faster – we're working smarter. The new system allows us to be more flexible, to switch between product lines with minimal downtime. We're more responsive to customer needs than ever before."

Richard listened intently, his brow furrowed in concentration. Bob could almost see the gears turning in the chairman's head, calculating the potential impact on their bottom line.

As they continued their tour, Bob and Alex took turns explaining the various initiatives underway – the cross-functional teams, the Heritage Innovation project, the sustainability efforts. With each stop, Richard's skepticism seemed to wane, replaced by a growing sense of cautious optimism.

Their final stop was Bob's office, where the memory wall had been expanded to include excerpts from Rhys Morgan's journal and blueprints. Richard stood before it, his eyes scanning the wealth of historical innovation laid out before him.

"I had no idea," he murmured, almost to himself. "All this history, this legacy of innovation... it's remarkable."

Bob seized the moment. "Richard, what you're seeing here is more than just our past. It's the foundation for our future. We're not just changing for the sake of change. We're reconnecting with the innovative spirit that's always been at the heart of Maple and Brick."

Alex stepped forward, her voice calm but passionate. "Mr. Hawthorne, transformation is never easy, and it's rarely a straight line from A to B. But what we're doing here isn't just about survival – it's about positioning Maple and Brick to thrive in a rapidly changing world."

Richard was quiet for a long moment, his gaze still fixed on the memory wall. Finally, he turned to face Bob and Alex. "I came here today prepared to put a stop to all this," he admitted. "The board has been pressuring me to rein in these 'experimental' initiatives and focus on short-term profits."

Bob felt his heart sink, but Richard wasn't finished.

"However," the chairman continued, "what I've seen today has given me pause. You're not just innovating, you're evolving. You're honoring Maple and Brick's legacy while pushing into new frontiers." He paused, a small smile playing at the corners of his mouth. "I think I need to have a conversation with the rest of the board. You may have just gained an ally, Bob."

As Richard left, promising to be in touch soon, Bob felt a wave of relief wash over him. He turned to Alex, who was beaming. "That went better than I could have hoped," he said.

Alex nodded, her eyes twinkling. "Sometimes, Bob, our greatest adversaries can become our strongest allies. All it takes is a shift in perspective."

The rest of the day passed in a blur of activity. News of Richard's visit spread quickly, and there was a palpable sense of excitement in the air. The transformation efforts, which had sometimes felt like an uphill battle, suddenly seemed more achievable, more real.

However, not everyone was thrilled with the new developments. As Bob made his rounds in the afternoon, he overheard a heated conversation between Laura from marketing and Jacob from shipping.

"I'm telling you, Jacob, this is a mistake," Laura was saying, her voice tense. "We're alienating our core customers with all these new 'innovations'. They want reliability, not experiments."

Jacob shook his head, frustration evident in his voice. "Laura, can't you see that we need to evolve? Our old ways weren't sustainable. If we don't change, we'll be left behind."

Bob was about to intervene when Alex appeared at his side, placing a gentle hand on his arm. "Let them work it out," she murmured. "This kind of tension is normal in a transformation process. It's how we handle it that matters."

As they watched, Emily joined the conversation, bringing a fresh perspective. Slowly, the tension began to dissipate as the three colleagues started to find common ground, discussing ways to balance innovation with customer needs.

Later that evening, as the factory wound down for the day, Bob found himself once again standing beneath the old maple tree. The setting sun cast long shadows across the parking lot, and a cool breeze rustled through the leaves above.

Alex joined him, her presence a comforting constant in the whirlwind of change. "Quite a day," she remarked, her voice soft.

Bob nodded, his mind still processing everything that had happened. "I never expected Richard to become an ally," he admitted. "And I'm worried about the resistance we're still seeing from some quarters."

Alex smiled, her gaze fixed on the factory before them. "Transformation is never a smooth road, Bob. There will always be allies and adversaries, sometimes within the same person. The key is to keep moving forward, to keep communicating, to keep showing people the vision of what's possible."

As if on cue, they saw Laura, Jacob, and Emily exiting the factory together, deep in conversation. Despite their earlier disagreement, they seemed united now, gesturing animatedly as they discussed some new idea.

"You see?" Alex said, nodding towards the trio. "Even our adversaries can become allies when they're given the chance to be part of the solution."

Bob felt a renewed sense of hope and determination wash over him. Yes, there were still challenges ahead. Yes, there would be more resistance to overcome, more adversaries to convert. But they were making progress, step by step, day by day.

As the last light faded from the sky, Bob turned to Alex. "You know, when we started this journey, I thought it was about saving a company. But it's become so much more than that. We're not just transforming Maple and Brick – we're transforming ourselves, our community, maybe even our entire industry."

Alex nodded, a proud smile on her face. "That's the true power of transformation, Bob. It ripples outward, touching everything and everyone in its path. And it all starts with one person willing to take that first step, to be the catalyst for change."

As they walked back towards the factory, Bob felt a surge of gratitude – for Alex's guidance, for his team's dedication, for the legacy of innovation that had brought them to this point. The road ahead was still long and uncertain, but he no longer felt alone on the journey.

The next morning dawned bright and clear, a new day full of possibilities. As Bob drove to the factory, he noticed something that made him smile. The "For Sale" sign that had once stood at the edge of the property, a grim reminder of how close they had come to failure, was gone. In its place was a new sign:

"Maple and Brick Manufacturing: Honoring Our Past, Innovating for the Future"

It was a small change, but it felt significant. It was a declaration of intent, a statement of purpose. They weren't just fighting for survival anymore – they were building something new, something lasting.

As Bob parked his car and made his way to the entrance, he saw his team gathering for the start of another day. There was Joe, sharing a laugh with Mike as they discussed some new idea for the production line. Emily was deep in conversation with Laura, no doubt finding ways to align their sustainability initiatives with market demands. Jacob was demonstrating a new feature of the inventory system to a group of interested colleagues.

And there, in the midst of it all, was Alex, her presence a catalyst for creativity and collaboration. She caught Bob's eye and smiled, giving him a small nod of encouragement.

Bob took a deep breath, feeling the weight of responsibility but also the thrill of possibility. They had allies now – in Richard, in each other, in the very history of Maple and Brick. And even their adversaries were becoming partners in the journey of transformation.

As he stepped through the factory doors, ready to face whatever challenges the day might bring, Bob felt a sense of certainty settle over him. They were on the right path. The winds of change were no longer just a force to be weathered – they were the very thing propelling Maple and Brick into a bright and innovative future.

The transformation continued, and with each passing day, the line between allies and adversaries blurred a little more. They were becoming something greater than the sum of their parts – a true community of innovators, bound together by a shared vision and a commitment to honoring the past while fearlessly embracing the future.

And in that unity, in that shared purpose, lay the true strength of Maple and Brick. It was more than a company now – it was a movement, a testament to the power of transformation to not just change a business, but to change lives, to change an industry, to change the world.

The journey was far from over, but with allies old and new by their side, Bob knew that Maple and Brick was ready for whatever lay ahead.

The spirit of innovation that had seen them through countless challenges in the past was alive and well, burning brighter than ever before.

And as the factory came to life around him, humming with the energy of possibility, Bob Harrington smiled. The best was yet to come.

CHAPTER 8 REFLECTION: ALLIES AND ADVERSARIES

Key Insights:
- ❖ Transformation often reveals both unexpected allies and adversaries.
- ❖ Building alliances and addressing opposition head-on are key to navigating change.

Personal Reflection:

Who have been your most valuable allies in recent endeavors? Conversely, where have you encountered unexpected opposition? How did these relationships impact your progress?

Application Question:

How can you cultivate stronger alliances to support your goals, and how might you turn potential adversaries into partners in your journey toward change?

Action Step:

Identify one potential ally you haven't fully engaged and one adversary you've been avoiding. Plan a conversation with each to strengthen your support network and address concerns.

Quote to Remember:

"In the crucible of transformation, we discover who stands with us and who stands against us — and sometimes, those lines blur in surprising ways."

CHAPTER 9:
THE POINT OF NO RETURN

The crisp autumn air carried a sense of anticipation as Bob Harrington made his way to Maple and Brick. The trees lining the street were ablaze with color, their leaves a vibrant tapestry of red, gold, and orange. It seemed fitting, Bob thought, that nature itself was undergoing a transformation as their company stood on the brink of its own metamorphosis.

Today marked a crucial milestone in their journey. The board was convening for a special meeting to review the progress of their transformation efforts and to make a decision that would shape the future of Maple and Brick. Bob knew that by the end of the day, they would either be fully committed to their new path or forced to abandon their vision and revert to old ways.

As he approached the factory, Bob saw Alex Chen waiting for him at the entrance. Her usual calm demeanor was tinged with a hint of nervous energy.

"Good morning, Bob," she greeted him. "Are you ready for today?"

Bob took a deep breath, squaring his shoulders. "As ready as I'll ever be. This is it, isn't it? The point of no return."

Alex nodded, her eyes shining with determination. "Indeed it is. But remember, Bob, we've come so far already. The seeds of change we've planted are already starting to bear fruit. Now it's time to show the board just how much we've grown."

They made their way inside, where the factory was already humming with activity. The energy in the air was palpable — a mix of excitement and anxiety that seemed to touch everyone they passed.

In the conference room, Bob's core team was gathered, making last-minute preparations for their presentations. Emily was rehearsing her pitch on the nanoparticle-enhanced polymers, while Jacob fine-tuned his report on the new inventory management system. Joe and Mike huddled over production data, their earlier antagonism replaced by a shared focus on showcasing their achievements.

Laura, who had once been their most vocal skeptic, was now passionately outlining the market potential of their Heritage Innovation line. "We're not just selling products," she was saying to no one in particular. "We're selling a piece of American manufacturing history, reimagined for the future."

Bob felt a surge of pride as he watched his team. They had come so far, overcome so much. But would it be enough to convince the board?

As the hour of the meeting approached, board members began to arrive. Bob greeted each one, trying to gauge their mood. Some seemed cautiously optimistic, while others wore expressions of skepticism. Richard Hawthorne, their unexpected ally from the previous visit, offered Bob an encouraging nod as he took his seat.

Once everyone was settled, Bob stood to address the room. He could feel the weight of expectation pressing down on him, but he drew strength from the presence of his team and from the legacy of innovation that had brought them to this point.

"Ladies and gentlemen of the board," he began, his voice steady despite the butterflies in his stomach, "thank you for being here today. Three months ago, we stood at a crossroads. Maple and Brick was facing obsolescence, struggling to compete in a rapidly changing market. We made the bold decision to embark on a journey of transformation, to reconnect with our innovative roots and reimagine what we could be."

He paused, looking around the room. "Today, we're here to show you the fruits of that decision. But before we dive into the specifics, I want to remind you all of something. Maple and Brick has always been more than just a company. We're a legacy, a community, a symbol of American ingenuity and resilience. What we're doing now isn't just about survival – it's about honoring that legacy by ensuring we remain at the forefront of innovation for generations to come."

With that, Bob handed the floor over to his team. One by one, they presented their initiatives, their achievements, and their visions for the future.

Emily wowed the board with her nanoparticle-enhanced polymers, demonstrating their incredible strength-to-weight ratio and biodegradability. "This isn't just a new product," she explained. "It's a whole new category of materials that could revolutionize industries from medical devices to aerospace."

Jacob and Joe tag-teamed their presentation on the optimized production processes. They showed how their blend of cutting-edge technology and time-tested craftsmanship had not only increased efficiency but also improved quality and reduced waste. "We're not just making things faster," Joe said, his gruff voice filled with pride. "We're making them better."

Laura's presentation on the Heritage Innovation line drew audible gasps of appreciation from several board members. She showcased prototypes of products that seamlessly blended Maple and Brick's rich history with modern technology – smart home devices housed in casings inspired by vintage radio designs, high-performance outdoor gear that echoed the rugged spirit of early New England settlers.

"These aren't just products," Laura said, her eyes shining. "They're stories. They're connections to our past and bridges to our future. And our market research shows that there's a huge appetite for this kind of meaningful innovation."

Throughout the presentations, Bob watched the board members' reactions closely. He saw skepticism give way to interest, and interest blossom into excitement. Even the most doubtful among them seemed to be coming around.

Finally, it was Alex's turn to speak. She stood, commanding the room's attention with her quiet confidence.

"What you've seen today is more than just a collection of new products or processes," she began. "It's evidence of a fundamental shift in how Maple and Brick operates. We've broken down silos, fostered collaboration, and reignited the spirit of innovation that has always been at the heart of this company."

She clicked to a slide showing key performance indicators. "In just three months, we've seen a 22% increase in production efficiency, a 15% reduction in waste, and early market testing of our new product lines shows potential for a 30% increase in market share within the first year."

The room buzzed with murmurs of approval, but Alex wasn't finished. "But perhaps the most important metric isn't something that can be easily quantified. It's the change in culture, the renewed sense of purpose and pride that you can feel the moment you step onto the factory floor."

As Alex concluded her presentation, a heavy silence fell over the room. Bob stood, his heart pounding. "Ladies and gentlemen, what we're proposing today isn't just a new direction for Maple and Brick. It's a commitment to continuous innovation, to adaptive resilience, to being a leader rather than a follower in our industry. We're asking for your full support to continue down this path of transformation. We believe it's not just the right choice – it's the only choice if we want to secure Maple and Brick's future for generations to come."

The board chairman, a stern-faced man named Harold Winters, leaned forward. "This is all very impressive, Bob. But it's also risky. How can we be sure this isn't just a flash in the pan? How do we know these changes will stick?"

Bob was about to respond when, to his surprise, Richard Hawthorne spoke up. "Harold, I had the same concerns when I first heard about these initiatives. But I've seen firsthand the changes taking place at Maple and Brick. This isn't just about new products or processes. It's about a fundamental shift in how the company operates, how it thinks about itself and its place in the world."

Another board member, Janet Lee, chimed in. "I agree with Richard. The financials are promising, but what really strikes me is the energy, the sense of purpose. We're not just looking at a company that's changing – we're looking at a company that's learned how to change. That's invaluable in today's market."

As the discussion continued, Bob felt a glimmer of hope. The board members were engaged, asking thoughtful questions, and seeming genuinely excited about the possibilities.

Finally, after what felt like hours, Harold called for a vote. "All those in favor of fully supporting and funding the continuation of Maple and Brick's transformation initiatives, please say aye."

The room filled with a chorus of "ayes," with not a single voice in opposition.

Harold nodded, a small smile breaking through his usually stern demeanor. "Well, Bob, it seems you've convinced us. You have the board's full support to continue down this path. We'll be watching closely, but we're excited to see where this journey takes Maple and Brick."

As the meeting adjourned and the board members filed out, offering congratulations and words of encouragement, Bob felt a wave of emotion wash over him. They had done it. They had reached the point of no return and come out on the other side, committed to a new future for Maple and Brick.

Alex approached, her face beaming with pride. "Congratulations, Bob. You've just secured a new lease on life for Maple and Brick."

Bob shook his head, smiling. "We did this, Alex. All of us. I couldn't have done it without you, without the team, without everyone who believed in this vision."

As they made their way out of the conference room, they were met by a crowd of anxious employees who had been waiting to hear the news. Bob looked at their faces – hopeful, nervous, expectant – and felt the weight of their trust in him.

"Well?" Joe called out, his gruff voice cutting through the tension. "Don't keep us in suspense, Mr. Harrington. What did the board say?"

Bob paused for a moment, drawing out the suspense, then broke into a wide grin. "They said yes. We have their full support to continue our transformation journey."

The hallway erupted in cheers. People were hugging, high-fiving, some even wiping away tears of relief and joy. Bob saw Emily and Jacob embracing, their earlier conflicts forgotten in the face of this shared victory. Laura was already on her phone, no doubt eager to share the news with their marketing partners.

As the celebration continued around him, Bob slipped away, making his way outside to the old maple tree. The late afternoon sun filtered through its leaves, casting dappled shadows on the ground. He placed a hand on its rough bark, feeling a connection to all those who had stood in this spot before him, facing their own challenges and making their own bold decisions.

Alex joined him a few moments later, her presence a quiet comfort. "How does it feel, Bob?" she asked softly. "To have crossed the point of no return?"

Bob was quiet for a moment, considering her question. "It feels... right," he said finally. "Like we're exactly where we're supposed to be. But it also feels like a beginning, not an end. We've committed to this path of continuous transformation. The real work starts now."

Alex nodded, her eyes shining with approval. "That's exactly the right mindset, Bob. This isn't a destination – it's a journey. But it's one that Maple and Brick is now equipped to undertake."

As they stood there, the sounds of celebration drifting out from the factory, Bob felt a profound sense of gratitude and purpose. They had honored the legacy of Maple and Brick not by clinging to the past, but by using it as a foundation to build a bold new future.

The point of no return had been crossed. There would be new challenges ahead, new obstacles to overcome. But they would face them together, as a team, as a community, as Maple and Brick reborn.

As the sun began to set, painting the sky in brilliant hues of orange and pink, Bob took one last look at the factory before heading home. The old brick walls seemed to glow in the fading light, a testament to the enduring strength of Maple and Brick. But now, those walls didn't just represent the past – they were the canvas upon which a new future would be painted.

Tomorrow would bring new tasks, new goals, new mountains to climb. But for now, in this moment, Bob allowed himself to savor the victory. They had taken a leap of faith, and landed on solid ground. The transformation of Maple and Brick was no longer just a possibility – it was a reality, a commitment, a promise to themselves and to the future.

As he drove home, Bob's mind was already racing with ideas for their next steps. The point of no return was behind them, and the horizon ahead was limitless. Maple and Brick was ready to write the next chapter in its long and storied history, and Bob Harrington was proud to be holding the pen.

CHAPTER 9 REFLECTION: THE POINT OF NO RETURN

Key Insights:
- ❖ Every transformative journey reaches a critical juncture where turning back is no longer an option.
- ❖ Embracing this point of no return requires courage and unwavering commitment to the vision.

Personal Reflection:
Recall a time when you crossed a point of no return in a project or major life decision. What gave you the courage to push forward despite the risks and uncertainties?

Application Question:
How can you prepare yourself and your team for those critical moments when there's no turning back? What resources or mindsets do you need to cultivate?

Action Step:
Identify the "point of no return" in your current major initiative. Create a commitment statement outlining why pushing forward is essential and what you're willing to risk to succeed.

Quote to Remember:
"At the point of no return, we find our true resolve and the strength to forge ahead into uncharted territories."

CHAPTER 10: CRISIS AND OPPORTUNITY

The early winter chill nipped at Bob Harrington's face as he hurried towards Maple and Brick. The factory loomed ahead, its brick façade dusted with a light coating of frost. It had been two months since the board's unanimous decision to support their transformation efforts, and the initial euphoria had given way to the hard work of implementing their ambitious plans.

As Bob approached the entrance, he noticed an unusual flurry of activity. Employees were rushing in and out, their faces etched with worry. His phone buzzed in his pocket – a message from Alex: "Emergency in the production line. Meet me there ASAP."

Bob's heart raced as he quickened his pace. They had made so much progress, but he knew that in the world of manufacturing, a single crisis could unravel months of hard work.

As he burst through the factory doors, the usual hum of machinery was replaced by an eerie silence. He found Alex, Joe, and Mike huddled around the main production line, which stood motionless.

"What happened?" Bob asked, trying to keep the panic out of his voice.

Joe turned to him, his face grim. "It's the new AI-driven system, Mr. Harrington. It's gone haywire. Started producing defective parts and then shut down completely. We can't get it to restart."

Mike chimed in, his usual enthusiasm dampened by stress. "We've been trying to troubleshoot for the past hour, but nothing's working. It's like the system's locked us out."

Bob felt a knot form in his stomach. This was exactly the kind of setback they couldn't afford. "How long until we can get it back up and running?"

Alex shook her head. "That's the problem, Bob. We don't know. This system is so new, so complex – it could take days to diagnose and fix the issue."

The implications hit Bob like a ton of bricks. Days of lost production. Missed deadlines. Angry customers. All the goodwill and momentum they had built over the past months could evaporate in an instant.

As if reading his mind, Laura appeared at his side, her face pale with worry. "Bob, I've already gotten calls from three major clients. They're demanding answers, threatening to cancel orders. What do I tell them?"

For a moment, Bob felt overwhelmed by the magnitude of the crisis. But then he remembered the words of his great-grandfather Rhys, written in that old journal: "In times of crisis, look not just at the problem, but at the opportunity it presents."

Taking a deep breath, Bob addressed the group. "Alright, here's what we're going to do. Joe, Mike – I want you to assemble a team to work on getting the AI system back online. But also, start prepping our old production line as a backup."

Joe nodded, a glimmer of relief in his eyes at the thought of returning to familiar territory.

"Laura," Bob continued, "full transparency with our clients. Tell them we've hit a snag, but we're working on it. Offer them a choice – wait for us to resolve this and get a discount, or we'll produce their orders on our legacy system at the regular price."

Laura raised an eyebrow. "You think that'll work?"

"It gives them control," Alex interjected, nodding approvingly at Bob. "People are more understanding of delays when they feel they have a choice in the matter."

"Exactly," Bob agreed. "Now, where's Emily?"

As if on cue, Emily burst into the room, her lab coat fluttering behind her. "I think I might have a solution!" she exclaimed, her eyes bright with excitement despite the crisis around them.

All eyes turned to her as she continued, "Remember that small batch production system we've been developing on the side? The one that uses modular, reconfigurable units? I think we could adapt it to handle some of our most urgent orders while we fix the main line."

Bob felt a spark of hope ignite in his chest. "How quickly can we get it set up?"

Emily's brow furrowed in concentration. "With a full team working on it? Maybe 48 hours to get the first unit operational."

"Do it," Bob said without hesitation. "Pull whatever resources you need."

As the team dispersed to their tasks, Bob turned to Alex. "We need to get ahead of this. Call a company-wide meeting in an hour. Everyone needs to know what's happening and how we're responding."

Alex nodded, already pulling out her phone to send out the notification.

The next few hours were a whirlwind of activity. Bob moved from department to department, coordinating efforts, offering encouragement, and making quick decisions as new challenges arose.

By the time the company-wide meeting rolled around, the initial panic had given way to a focused determination. Employees filed into the main assembly area, their faces a mix of concern and curiosity.

Bob stood before them, acutely aware of the weight of their expectations. "I know many of you have heard about the crisis we're facing with our main production line," he began. "I'm not going to sugarcoat it – this is a serious setback. But I want you all to understand something. This is not just a crisis; it's an opportunity."

He paused, letting his words sink in. "An opportunity to prove that the changes we've been making aren't just surface level. An opportunity to show that Maple and Brick isn't just a company that can produce goods, but one that can innovate, adapt, and overcome in the face of adversity."

Bob went on to outline their multi-pronged approach: the team working to fix the AI system, the preparation of the legacy production line as a backup, and Emily's innovative solution with the modular production units.

"But here's where we need all of you," Bob continued. "This isn't just a challenge for our production team or our engineers. This is a moment for every single person at Maple and Brick to step up, to think creatively, to find ways to support our efforts and keep our promises to our customers."

As he spoke, Bob could see the mood in the room shifting. The fear and uncertainty were being replaced by a sense of purpose, of shared responsibility.

"Remember," Bob said, his voice filled with conviction, "we are the heirs to a legacy of innovation and resilience. Our predecessors faced world wars, economic depressions, and technological revolutions. They didn't just survive; they thrived. Now it's our turn to show what we're made of."

As the meeting concluded and employees returned to their tasks with renewed energy, Bob felt a hand on his shoulder. It was Joe, the grizzled veteran who had seen Maple and Brick through countless challenges over the decades.

"You know, Mr. Harrington," Joe said, his voice gruff but warm, "I've been through a lot of crises here. Seen a lot of leaders come and go. But I've never seen anyone handle it quite like you just did. You didn't just give orders; you gave us a reason to believe."

Bob felt a lump form in his throat at Joe's words. "Thank you, Joe. That means a lot coming from you."

As the day wore on, the factory buzzed with a new kind of energy. In every corner, people were stepping up, offering ideas, taking on new responsibilities. Emily's team worked around the clock to get the modular production units up and running. Laura and her team transformed into a crisis communication hub, keeping clients updated and even managing to secure a few expressions of support and admiration for Maple and Brick's transparent and innovative approach to the crisis.

By the end of the second day, they had their first victory. Emily's modular production unit came online, allowing them to start fulfilling their most urgent orders. The sight of the first perfectly formed components rolling off the new line sent a cheer through the factory.

On the third day, there was another breakthrough. Mike, working with a team that included both seasoned veterans and young tech enthusiasts, managed to isolate the bug in the AI system. By the end of the day, the main production line hummed back to life, more stable and efficient than ever.

As Bob made his rounds, he was struck by the transformation he was witnessing. People who had once been resistant to change were now eagerly embracing new ideas. Departments that had previously operated in silos were collaborating seamlessly. The crisis had forced them to live their values of innovation and adaptability, and they had risen to the challenge magnificently.

A week after the crisis began, Bob stood in his office, looking out over the factory floor. The main production line was back at full capacity, complemented by Emily's modular units which had proven so successful that they were now being integrated into their regular operations. The low hum of machinery was punctuated by the sounds of conversation and occasional laughter – a far cry from the tense silence of a week ago.

Alex joined him at the window, a smile playing on her lips. "You know, Bob, I've guided a lot of companies through transformation processes.

But I've never seen one come together quite like this. You should be proud."

Bob nodded, feeling a complex mix of emotions – pride, gratitude, and a deep sense of responsibility. "We've come a long way," he agreed. "But we can't rest on our laurels. This crisis showed us both our strengths and our vulnerabilities. We need to learn from it, to keep pushing forward."

"Absolutely," Alex said. "In fact, I think this experience has given us a unique opportunity. We've seen what this team is capable of when the chips are down. Now, how do we maintain that level of innovation and collaboration in our day-to-day operations?"

As they discussed ideas, Bob's phone buzzed with a message. It was from Richard Hawthorne, the board chairman: "Bob, the board has been briefed on how you handled the recent crisis. We're impressed. Very impressed. We'd like to discuss expanding the transformation budget at the next meeting. Keep up the good work."

Bob showed the message to Alex, a grin spreading across his face. "Well, how's that for turning a crisis into an opportunity?"

Alex laughed, her eyes twinkling. "I'd say Maple and Brick is living up to its legacy of innovation and resilience. Your great-grandfather would be proud."

As the day drew to a close, Bob made one last round of the factory. He stopped to chat with Joe, who was showing a group of younger workers how to fine-tune the newly restarted production line. He peeked into the R&D lab, where Emily and her team were already exploring new applications for their modular production system. He passed by Laura's office, overhearing her on the phone with a client, confidently discussing how Maple and Brick's handling of the crisis demonstrated their commitment to innovation and customer service.

Finally, Bob found himself once again under the old maple tree outside the factory. The winter wind whistled through its bare branches, but Bob felt a warmth inside him that no chill could touch. They had faced a crisis and come out stronger. They had turned a potential disaster into an opportunity for growth and innovation.

As he turned to head home, Bob's gaze fell on the factory. In the gathering dusk, the warm glow of lights from within gave it an almost magical quality. This wasn't just a building of brick and metal; it was a crucible of innovation, a testament to human resilience and creativity.

The crisis had tested them, pushed them to their limits. But in doing so, it had also revealed the true strength of Maple and Brick – not in its machines or its processes, but in its people. In their ability to come together, to innovate, to persevere in the face of adversity.

As Bob got into his car, he felt a renewed sense of purpose and excitement. They had weathered this storm, but he knew there would be others. Yet now, he faced the future not with fear, but with confidence. Whatever challenges lay ahead, Maple and Brick would meet them head-on, turning each crisis into an opportunity, each setback into a stepping stone towards a brighter future.

The transformation journey continued, and Maple and Brick was stronger than ever, ready to write the next chapter in its storied history.

CHAPTER 10 REFLECTION: CRISIS AND OPPORTUNITY

Key Insights:
- Every crisis contains within it the seeds of opportunity for growth and innovation.
- How we respond to adversity often defines the outcome of our journey.

Personal Reflection:

Think about a significant crisis you've faced in your personal or professional life. What unexpected opportunities emerged from this challenging situation? How did you recognize and seize these opportunities?

Application Question:

How can you develop a mindset that better recognizes and capitalizes on opportunities, even in the midst of crisis or adversity?

Action Step:

Create a "crisis opportunity" framework for yourself or your team. List potential crises you might face and brainstorm possible opportunities each could present.

Quote to Remember:

"In the depths of crisis, we often find the greatest opportunities for transformation and growth."

CHAPTER 11:
THE DARK NIGHT OF THE SOUL

The winter storm howled outside, its icy fingers seeming to claw at the windows of Maple and Brick. Inside his office, Bob Harrington sat alone, the soft glow of his desk lamp creating a small island of light in the darkness. It was well past midnight, but sleep eluded him as he pored over financial reports and production data.

The euphoria of overcoming the production line crisis had faded, replaced by a gnawing anxiety that had been growing over the past few weeks. Despite their innovative solutions and the board's increased support, the numbers weren't adding up. The costs of their transformation were mounting, and the promised returns were taking longer to materialize than they had anticipated.

Bob rubbed his tired eyes, his gaze falling on the framed photo of his great-grandfather, Rhys Morgan. "What would you do?" he murmured, not for the first time. The weight of Maple and Brick's legacy, of the generations of workers who had called this place home, pressed down on him like a physical force.

A knock at the door startled him from his reverie. Alex Chen entered, her face etched with concern. "Bob? I saw the light on. What are you doing here so late?"

Bob gestured wearily at the papers strewn across his desk. "Trying to make sense of all this. Alex, I'm worried. We're burning through our transformation budget faster than expected, and we're not seeing the returns we projected. If we don't turn this around soon..."

He couldn't bring himself to finish the sentence, but Alex understood. She pulled up a chair, her expression somber. "I know, Bob. I've been crunching the numbers too. We're at a critical juncture."

For the next hour, they pored over the data together, exploring options, running scenarios. But with each calculation, the pit in Bob's stomach grew deeper. They had come so far, overcome so much. Could it all have been for nothing?

As the first light of dawn began to seep through the windows, Bob made a decision. "We need to call an emergency meeting. The whole team. We need to lay all our cards on the table."

Alex nodded, her face a mixture of concern and determination. "I agree. We're all in this together, Bob. Whatever comes next, we face it as a team."

The day that followed was one of the longest in Bob's life. As the core team gathered in the conference room, he could see the worry etched on each face. Emily, usually bubbling with enthusiasm, was uncharacteristically quiet. Joe's brow was furrowed deeply, his years of experience telling him that something was seriously wrong. Laura and Jacob exchanged nervous glances, sensing the gravity of the situation.

Bob took a deep breath and began to speak. He laid out the financial realities they were facing, not sugar-coating anything. The room grew increasingly tense as he explained that without a significant turnaround, they might be forced to scale back their transformation efforts dramatically – or worse.

"I'm not going to lie to you," Bob said, his voice heavy. "We're in a tough spot. The next few weeks will determine the future of Maple and Brick. I need ideas, I need solutions, and I need them fast."

The silence that followed was deafening. For a moment, Bob feared that the weight of the challenge had crushed the spirit of innovation they had worked so hard to cultivate.

But then, slowly, voices began to rise. Ideas were proposed, debated, refined. Emily suggested accelerating the development of their eco-friendly product line, arguing that the growing market for sustainable goods could provide a much-needed revenue boost. Jacob proposed a radical restructuring of their supply chain to cut costs without sacrificing quality. Laura outlined an aggressive marketing strategy to capitalize on the goodwill they had generated during the recent crisis.

As the discussion continued, Bob felt a glimmer of hope. The team was rallying, drawing on their collective knowledge and creativity to find a way forward. But he knew that ideas alone wouldn't be enough. They needed action, and they needed it now.

Over the next few days, Maple and Brick entered a state of controlled chaos. Every department was tasked with finding ways to cut costs and increase efficiency without compromising their transformation goals. Bob barely left the factory, catching quick naps on the couch in his office when exhaustion overtook him.

But despite their best efforts, setbacks continued to mount. A key client, nervous about the rumors of Maple and Brick's financial troubles, pulled a major order. A promising new product developed by Emily's team failed its final round of testing, forcing them back to the drawing board. The local newspaper ran a story speculating about potential layoffs, causing unrest among the workforce.

It was during this dark time that Bob found himself once again standing beneath the old maple tree, its bare branches stark against the gray winter sky. He felt hollowed out, drained of the optimism and determination that had carried him this far.

"I don't know if I can do this," he whispered to the wind. "I don't know if I'm the right person to lead Maple and Brick through this."

As if in answer, a gust of wind shook the tree, sending a shower of snow cascading down around him. Among the swirling flakes, Bob caught a glimpse of green – a single leaf that had somehow clung to its branch through the winter, a stubborn reminder of life and growth even in the harshest conditions.

The sight stirred something in Bob's memory. He rushed back to his office, pulling out the old journal of his great-grandfather. Flipping through the pages, he found what he was looking for – an entry from the depths of the Great Depression:

"These are dark days for Maple and Brick. The economy is in shambles, orders have dried up, and I fear for the future of this company and the families that depend on it. But I am reminded of the old maple tree outside. Year after year, it weathers the harshest winters, only to bloom anew in the spring. We too must find that resilience within ourselves. Our challenges are great, but our spirit is greater. We will endure. We will innovate. We will grow again."

Bob read the words over and over, feeling a connection to his ancestor that transcended time. Rhys had faced challenges that seemed insurmountable, yet he had persevered. Maple and Brick had survived and thrived because of that unyielding spirit. As he contemplated the challenges ahead, Bob found himself wishing he could tap into the creative energy that had drawn artists and writer to the nearby MacDowell Colony for over a century. The tranquil grounds had inspired the likes of Thorton Wilder and Aaron Copland.

With renewed determination, Bob called the team together once more. But this time, instead of focusing on financial projections and market analyses, he shared Rhys's journal entry with them. He spoke of the legacy of resilience and innovation that ran through the very foundations of Maple and Brick.

"We've been so focused on the numbers, on the short-term challenges, that we've lost sight of who we are," Bob said, his voice growing stronger with each word. "We are not just a company. We are a community. We are innovators. We are problem-solvers. And right now, we have the biggest problem of our lives to solve."

He looked around the room, meeting each person's gaze. "I can't promise you that the road ahead will be easy. But I can promise you this: if we stand together, if we draw on the strength and creativity that has always been the heart of Maple and Brick, we will find a way through this dark night."

As Bob spoke, he could see a change coming over the team. The despair and resignation that had begun to settle in was being replaced by a fierce determination. They had not come this far, had not worked so hard, to give up now.

Over the next weeks, Maple and Brick underwent a transformation unlike anything they had planned. Every aspect of the company was re-examined, every process scrutinized. But this time, it wasn't just about cutting costs or increasing efficiency. It was about rediscovering their core identity, about innovating not just their products but their entire approach to business.

Emily's team, freed from the pressure of quick returns, made a breakthrough in their eco-friendly materials research that opened up entirely new market possibilities. Joe and the production team found ways to blend their new high-tech systems with time-tested manufacturing techniques, creating a hybrid approach that was both more efficient and more flexible than either method alone. Laura launched a marketing campaign that didn't just promote their products but told the story of Maple and Brick's resilience and commitment to innovation, striking a chord with consumers looking for authenticity in an increasingly corporate world.

Slowly but surely, the tide began to turn. Orders started to pick up. Costs, while still high, began to stabilize. The energy in the factory, which had been somber and tense, became charged with a sense of shared purpose and possibility.

As spring began to stir outside, bringing new life to the old maple tree, Bob stood in his office, looking out over the factory floor. The past months had been the greatest challenge of his life, a true dark night of the soul. But they had emerged from it stronger, more unified, more certain of their identity and purpose than ever before.

Alex joined him at the window, a smile playing on her lips. "You know, Bob, in all my years of consulting, I've never seen a company go through a transformation quite like this. You should be proud."

Bob shook his head, his eyes still on the busy factory floor below. "I'm not proud of myself, Alex. I'm proud of them. Every single person down there. They're the ones who brought us through this dark night. They're the true heart and soul of Maple and Brick."

As they stood there, watching the hum of activity below, Bob felt a deep sense of gratitude and purpose wash over him. They had faced their darkest hour and come through it not just intact, but renewed. The challenges weren't over – they never would be in the ever-changing world of business. But now, Bob knew with certainty that whatever the future held, Maple and Brick would face it together, drawing strength from their past to innovate for their future.

The dark night of the soul had passed, and a new dawn was breaking for Maple and Brick. The transformation continued, not as a finite project, but as an ongoing journey of growth, innovation, and resilience. And in that journey lay the true legacy of Maple and Brick – a legacy not just of products made, but of lives touched, of community strengthened, and of the enduring power of the human spirit to overcome even the darkest of nights.

CHAPTER 11 REFLECTION: THE DARK NIGHT OF THE SOUL

Key Insights:
- ❖ The darkest moments in a journey often precede the greatest breakthroughs.
- ❖ Resilience and perseverance through doubt and despair are crucial for transformation.

Personal Reflection:

Recall a time when you experienced a "dark night of the soul" in your work or personal life. How did you find the strength to push through? What did you learn about yourself in the process?

Application Question:

What strategies can you develop to maintain resilience and hope during the most challenging times of your transformative journey?

Action Step:

Create a personal resilience toolkit. Include practices, mantras, or resources you can turn to when facing moments of deep doubt or difficulty.

Quote to Remember:

"It is in our darkest moments that we must focus to see the light of possibility."

CHAPTER 12:
EMBRACING INNOVATION

The first warm breezes of spring whispered through the budding branches of the old maple tree as Bob Harrington approached Maple and Brick. The factory stood proudly against the brightening sky, its brick facade seeming to glow with renewed purpose. It had been two months since their darkest hour, and the energy of rebirth was palpable in the air.

As Bob entered the building, he was greeted by a flurry of activity. The main floor had been transformed into a makeshift exhibition space, with various stations showcasing new products, processes, and ideas. Today marked the launch of Maple and Brick's first-ever Innovation Fair, an internal event designed to celebrate and accelerate their commitment to creative problem-solving.

Emily rushed up to Bob, her eyes shining with excitement. "Mr. Harrington! You've got to see this. We've made a breakthrough with the nanoparticle-enhanced polymers. The latest tests show a 40% increase in tensile strength while maintaining full biodegradability!"

Bob followed her to a display where various samples of the new material were being put through their paces. He watched in amazement as a thin sheet of the polymer, no thicker than a playing card, effortlessly supported the weight of a bowling ball.

"This is incredible, Emily," Bob said, his mind already racing with potential applications. "Have you started exploring market possibilities?"

Emily nodded enthusiastically. "We've already had preliminary discussions with a medical device manufacturer. They're interested in using it for next-generation implants. And that's just the beginning. The aerospace industry, sustainable packaging, advanced textiles – the potential is enormous."

As they continued their tour, Bob was struck by the transformation he was witnessing. Every corner of the factory seemed to buzz with creative energy. In one area, Joe and Mike were demonstrating a hybrid production line that seamlessly blended traditional craftsmanship with cutting-edge robotics.

"You see, Mr. Harrington," Joe explained, his gruff voice tinged with pride, "we've programmed the robots to handle the repetitive, high-precision tasks, freeing up our skilled workers to focus on the areas where human judgment and experience really make a difference."

Mike chimed in, "And the best part is, the AI learns from our veteran craftsmen. It's not replacing them; it's preserving and amplifying their expertise."

Bob nodded approvingly, impressed by how they had managed to honor Maple and Brick's heritage while pushing the boundaries of modern manufacturing.

Moving on, he came across Jacob showcasing a revolutionary new inventory management system. "We've integrated blockchain technology with IoT sensors," Jacob explained, his words tumbling out in his excitement. "Every component, every product can be tracked in real-time from raw material to end-user. It's not just about efficiency; it's about transparency and sustainability."

Laura's marketing team had set up a virtual reality booth where visitors could take a tour through Maple and Brick's history, from its humble beginnings to its cutting-edge present. "We're not just selling products anymore," Laura said, her eyes alight with passion. "We're selling a story of American ingenuity and resilience. And people are responding. Our brand recognition has shot up 30% in the past month alone."

As Bob made his way through the fair, he felt a swelling of pride and excitement. This wasn't just a showcase of new products or processes. It was a testament to the spirit of innovation that had been rekindled at Maple and Brick. Every employee, from the newest hire to the most seasoned veteran, seemed energized and engaged.

Midway through the morning, Bob found himself back in his office with Alex, taking a moment to process everything they had seen.

"It's remarkable, isn't it?" Alex said, a smile playing on her lips. "A few months ago, we were fighting for survival. Now, we're on the cusp of a new era for Maple and Brick."

Bob nodded, his expression thoughtful. "It's more than I could have hoped for. But Alex, I can't help but wonder – how do we maintain this momentum? How do we ensure that innovation becomes a permanent part of our DNA, not just a response to crisis?"

Alex leaned forward, her eyes sparkling with the challenge. "That, Bob, is the million-dollar question. And I think I might have an idea."

Over the next hour, Alex outlined a bold new initiative. She proposed creating an "Innovation Incubator" within Maple and Brick – a dedicated space and program where employees from all departments could come together to work on blue-sky projects and radical new ideas.

"The key," Alex explained, "is to create a culture where innovation isn't just encouraged – it's expected. Where failure is seen not as a setback, but as a valuable learning experience. We need to give people the time, resources, and freedom to explore ideas that might seem crazy at first glance."

Bob listened intently, his mind racing with the possibilities. "It's risky," he said finally. "The board might balk at allocating resources to projects without a clear, immediate return on investment."

Alex nodded, acknowledging the concern. "It is risky. But so is standing still in a rapidly changing world. We need to make the case that this kind of structured innovation is an investment in Maple and Brick's long-term future."

As they continued to discuss the idea, refining and expanding it, Bob felt a growing sense of excitement. This wasn't just another initiative or program. It was a fundamental shift in how Maple and Brick approached innovation – a way to institutionalize the creative spirit that had seen them through their darkest hour.

By the end of the day, as the Innovation Fair wound down and employees began to head home, there was a palpable sense of anticipation in the air. Bob gathered the core team for a final debrief, sharing the broad strokes of the Innovation Incubator idea.

The response was overwhelmingly positive. Emily's eyes lit up at the possibility of having dedicated time and resources for blue-sky research. Joe, initially skeptical, warmed to the idea when Bob emphasized that the incubator would also focus on innovating traditional manufacturing techniques.

"We're not leaving our roots behind," Bob assured him. "We're finding new ways to honor and build on them."

Laura immediately began brainstorming ways to integrate the incubator into their brand story. "This isn't just about creating new products," she mused. "It's about positioning Maple and Brick as a thought leader in American manufacturing."

As the team continued to discuss and refine the idea, Bob felt a deep sense of satisfaction. They had come so far from those dark days just a few months ago. The spirit of innovation that had always been part of Maple and Brick's DNA had not just been rekindled – it was blazing brighter than ever.

Over the next few weeks, the Innovation Incubator began to take shape. A disused section of the factory was renovated, transformed into a flexible space that could adapt to the needs of various projects. State-of-the-art equipment was installed, from 3D printers and virtual reality rigs to traditional woodworking tools and metalworking stations.

But the heart of the incubator wasn't in its physical trappings. It was in the program they developed to nurture and channel the creative energies of Maple and Brick's workforce. Every employee, regardless of their position or department, was encouraged to submit ideas for projects. A rotating committee, made up of both senior leadership and rank-and-file workers, would review proposals and allocate resources.

The first round of projects selected for the incubator was a testament to the diverse talents and interests of Maple and Brick's workforce. There was a team working on developing smart textiles that could adapt to environmental conditions, drawing on the company's roots in the textile industry. Another group was exploring ways to use augmented reality to enhance traditional craftsmanship techniques. A third team was investigating the potential of mycelium-based materials as a sustainable alternative to plastics.

As Bob watched the incubator come to life, he was struck by the transformation he was witnessing. Employees who had once been resistant to change were now eagerly embracing new technologies and ideas. The silos between departments were breaking down as people from different backgrounds and disciplines came together to tackle complex challenges.

One afternoon, as Bob was giving a tour of the incubator to a group of potential investors, he overheard a conversation that made him pause. Joe, the veteran machinist, was deep in discussion with a young software engineer named Danielle. They were hunched over a workbench, examining what looked like a hybrid of an old-fashioned lathe and a computer-controlled milling machine.

"You see, Danielle," Joe was saying, his gruff voice filled with enthusiasm, "if we can integrate your AI algorithms with the kind of fine control we get from manual operation, we could revolutionize small-batch production. It's the best of both worlds – the precision of a computer with the intuition of a skilled craftsman."

Danielle nodded excitedly. "And if we add in some machine learning capabilities, the system could actually improve over time, learning from the techniques of our most experienced machinists!"

Bob smiled to himself as he moved on with the tour. This was exactly the kind of cross-pollination of ideas he had hoped for when they launched the incubator.

As the weeks turned into months, the impact of the Innovation Incubator began to ripple through every aspect of Maple and Brick. New products were moving from concept to market faster than ever before. Production processes were becoming more efficient and adaptable. Even the company culture was shifting, becoming more open, more collaborative, more willing to take calculated risks.

But perhaps the most significant change was in how Maple and Brick was perceived in the wider world. Industry publications began to take notice of the innovative work coming out of the old New England factory. Potential clients, attracted by the company's blend of traditional craftsmanship and cutting-edge technology, were reaching out in increasing numbers.

One crisp autumn morning, almost a year after their darkest hour, Bob stood beneath the old maple tree, its leaves now a blaze of red and gold. Alex joined him, a tablet in her hand and a smile on her face.

"Have you seen the latest numbers?" she asked, handing him the tablet.

Bob scrolled through the report, his eyes widening. Revenue was up 25% year-over-year. Employee satisfaction scores had reached an all-time high. The pipeline of new products and innovations was fuller than it had ever been.

"This is incredible," Bob said, shaking his head in wonder. "A year ago, we were on the brink of collapse. Now..."

"Now you're leading the charge into the future of American manufacturing," Alex finished for him. "Bob, what you've achieved here is remarkable. You haven't just saved Maple and Brick – you've reinvented it."

As they stood there, watching the autumn breeze send a shower of colorful leaves swirling around them, Bob felt a profound sense of gratitude and purpose. They had embraced innovation not as a one-time fix, but as a fundamental part of who they were as a company.

The journey wasn't over – in many ways, it was just beginning. There would be new challenges to face, new problems to solve. But now, Maple and Brick was ready. They had rediscovered their innovative spirit, honoring their past while fearlessly embracing the future.

As Bob turned to head back into the factory, he paused for a moment, placing his hand on the rough bark of the old maple tree. He thought of all the generations who had stood in this spot before him, facing their own challenges, making their own bold decisions.

"We did it," he whispered, as much to those past generations as to himself. "We found a way to keep growing, keep innovating. The legacy lives on."

With that, Bob squared his shoulders and walked back into the factory, ready to face whatever the future might bring. The spirit of innovation was alive and well at Maple and Brick, a beacon of possibility in a rapidly changing world. And in that spirit lay the promise of a bright future, not just for the company, but for the community it served and the industry it was helping to reshape.

The transformation of Maple and Brick continued, an ongoing journey of growth, innovation, and renewal. And in that journey, they had found their true strength – not in clinging to the past, but in using it as a foundation to build a bold and exciting future.

CHAPTER 12 REFLECTION: EMBRACING INNOVATION

Key Insights:

- ❖ Innovation thrives in environments that encourage creativity and experimentation.
- ❖ Embracing change requires a mindset open to new ideas and possibilities.

Personal Reflection:

How open are you to innovation in your work or personal life? What fears or barriers have held you back from fully embracing new ideas or methods?

Application Question:

How can you create a more innovative environment in your team, organization, or personal life? What structures or practices could you implement to foster creativity?

Action Step:

Implement an "innovation hour" in your weekly schedule. Dedicate this time to exploring new ideas, learning about emerging trends, or experimenting with novel approaches to existing problems.

Quote to Remember:

"Innovation is not just about new technologies; it's about reimagining what's possible with the resources at hand."

CHAPTER 13: TRIALS AND TRIBULATIONS

The crisp autumn air carried a hint of woodsmoke as Bob Harrington made his way to Maple and Brick. The factory stood silhouetted against the morning sky, its brick facade gleaming in the early light. It had been eighteen months since they'd embarked on their transformation journey, and while they'd made remarkable progress, Bob knew that the path of innovation was never smooth.

As he entered the building, the usual hum of activity was punctuated by raised voices coming from the direction of the Innovation Incubator. Bob quickened his pace, a knot of concern forming in his stomach.

He found Emily and Jacob in the midst of a heated argument, their faces flushed with frustration. Alex stood nearby, her expression a mix of concern and curiosity.

"What's going on here?" Bob asked, his voice cutting through the tension.

Emily turned to him, her eyes flashing. "Jacob's team is hogging all the resources for their smart textile project. My biodegradable polymer research is falling behind schedule because we can't get access to the equipment we need!"

Jacob bristled. "That's not fair! Our project has shown the most immediate market potential. We're just trying to capitalize on that momentum."

Bob held up his hands, calling for calm. "Alright, let's take a step back. This is exactly the kind of situation the incubator was designed to handle. Alex, can you facilitate a resource allocation meeting this afternoon?"

Alex nodded, already pulling out her tablet to schedule the meeting. As Emily and Jacob reluctantly agreed to table their argument until then, Bob couldn't help but feel a twinge of worry. The passion and drive that made their innovation efforts so successful could also lead to conflict if not properly managed.

His concerns only grew as he made his rounds through the factory. In the production area, he found Joe struggling with one of the new hybrid manufacturing systems. The old machinist's face was etched with frustration as he tried to calibrate the AI-assisted lathe.

"Damned machine won't cooperate," Joe grumbled as Bob approached. "I've been at this for hours, and it still can't replicate the precision we get with the old manual methods."

Bob watched as Joe made another attempt, only to have the machine produce a part that was slightly out of spec. He could see the toll this was taking on the veteran employee, whose pride in his craftsmanship had always been a cornerstone of Maple and Brick's quality.

"Joe," Bob said gently, "why don't you take a break? Maybe work with Mike to see if there's a way to better integrate your expertise into the AI's learning algorithms."

Joe nodded grudgingly, but Bob could see the doubt in his eyes. The challenge of blending traditional skills with cutting-edge technology was proving more difficult than they had anticipated.

As the day wore on, more issues came to light. Laura from marketing burst into Bob's office, her usual composure shaken. "We've got a problem," she announced without preamble. "One of our competitors is claiming that our new smart textile line infringes on their patent. They're threatening legal action."

Bob felt his heart sink. They had been so focused on innovation that they might have overlooked the complex landscape of intellectual property rights. "Get our legal team on it right away," he instructed Laura. "And start preparing a PR strategy in case this goes public."

By the time the afternoon resource allocation meeting rolled around, Bob felt like he was juggling a dozen flaming torches. As he sat at the head of the conference table, looking at the faces of his team – some excited, some frustrated, all showing signs of stress – he realized that their transformation journey had entered a new and challenging phase.

Alex kicked off the meeting with a summary of the various projects currently underway in the Innovation Incubator. As she spoke, Bob could see the passion and pride in his team's eyes. Despite the challenges, they had accomplished so much.

But when it came time to discuss resource allocation, the tensions that had been simmering beneath the surface boiled over.

"We need to prioritize projects with the most immediate market potential," Jacob argued. "The smart textile line could revolutionize the athletic wear industry. We can't afford to slow down now."

Emily shot back, "And what about long-term sustainability? The biodegradable polymer research might not have immediate payoff, but it's crucial for our future in an increasingly eco-conscious market."

Joe chimed in, his voice gruff with frustration. "All this talk of new products, but we're struggling to maintain quality on our existing lines. We need to allocate more resources to perfecting our manufacturing processes."

As the debate raged on, Bob found himself torn. Each argument had merit, and he could see the passion behind every perspective. This was the double-edged sword of the innovation culture they had fostered – it drove them forward, but it also led to competing visions of the future.

Finally, Bob held up his hand, calling for silence. "I want to thank everyone for their input," he began, his voice steady despite the turmoil he felt inside. "What I'm hearing is that we've become victims of our own success. We have more great ideas than we have resources to pursue them all."

He paused, looking each team member in the eye. "But we can't let this abundance of innovation turn into infighting. We're all on the same team, working towards the same goal – to secure a bright future for Maple and Brick."

Bob turned to Alex. "I think we need to revisit our project evaluation criteria. We need a more holistic approach that balances immediate market potential with long-term sustainability and manufacturing excellence."

Alex nodded, already jotting down notes. "We could implement a scoring system that takes into account multiple factors – market potential, sustainability, alignment with core competencies, resource requirements, and so on."

The team began to discuss this new approach, the earlier tension gradually giving way to collaborative problem-solving. By the end of the meeting, they had outlined a new framework for project evaluation and resource allocation that seemed to address everyone's concerns.

As the team filed out, Bob felt a mix of exhaustion and cautious optimism. They had navigated a difficult conversation and come out stronger for it. But he knew that this was just one of many challenges they would face on their ongoing journey of transformation.

The next few weeks were a whirlwind of activity as they implemented the new project evaluation system and worked to address the various issues that had arisen. Bob found himself constantly moving between different areas of the company, putting out fires and trying to keep everyone aligned with their overall vision.

In the production area, he worked closely with Joe and Mike to refine the AI-assisted manufacturing systems. They brought in experts in human-computer interaction to help design interfaces that better leveraged the skills of experienced craftsmen. Slowly but surely, they began to find the right balance between automation and human expertise.

The patent issue with the smart textiles turned out to be a false alarm – their legal team was able to demonstrate that Maple and Brick's technology was sufficiently distinct from their competitor's. But the scare served as a wake-up call, leading them to implement more rigorous intellectual property checks in their innovation process.

Perhaps the most significant challenge came from an unexpected quarter. As news of Maple and Brick's innovative efforts spread, they began to receive acquisition offers from larger corporations. The board, seeing the potential for a quick return on their investment in the transformation process, was seriously considering these offers.

When Bob learned of this, he felt as if the ground was shifting beneath his feet. Everything they had worked for, the culture of innovation they had built, the commitment to their community – it could all be lost if they were swallowed up by a corporate giant.

He called an emergency meeting with Alex and the core team to discuss the situation. The mood in the room was somber as Bob laid out the facts.

"I won't lie to you," he said, his voice heavy with emotion. "This is a serious threat to everything we've built. If we're acquired, there's no guarantee that the new owners will continue our transformation efforts or maintain our commitment to the community."

Emily spoke up, her voice trembling slightly. "But they can't just sell us off, can they? After everything we've accomplished?"

Bob sighed. "The board has a fiduciary responsibility to consider all options that could benefit the shareholders. And on paper, these offers look very attractive."

The room fell silent as the team grappled with this new challenge. It was Alex who finally broke the silence.

"Then we need to make our case," she said, her voice filled with determination. "We need to show the board and the shareholders that the long-term value of continuing our transformation journey far outweighs the short-term gain of an acquisition."

Bob nodded slowly, feeling a glimmer of hope. "You're right. But how do we do that?"

What followed was an intense brainstorming session that lasted well into the night. They pored over financial projections, market analyses, and innovation pipelines. They crafted arguments that went beyond mere numbers, touching on Maple and Brick's legacy, its role in the community, and its potential to lead the future of American manufacturing.

By the time the sun rose the next morning, they had outlined a comprehensive presentation for the board. But Bob knew that this would be the fight of their lives. Everything they had worked for hung in the balance.

The day of the board meeting arrived all too quickly. As Bob stood before the assembled board members, he felt the weight of Maple and Brick's entire history on his shoulders. He thought of all the generations who had worked within these walls, of the community that depended on them, of the promise of innovation that they were just beginning to fulfill.

Taking a deep breath, he began his presentation. He spoke of the remarkable progress they had made, of the culture of innovation they had fostered, of the exciting projects in their pipeline. But he also spoke of the challenges they had faced and overcome, of the lessons they had learned, of the resilience they had developed.

"Ladies and gentlemen," he concluded, his voice ringing with passion, "Maple and Brick is not just a company. It's a legacy, a community, a beacon of innovation in American manufacturing. The offers on the table may look attractive on paper, but they cannot capture the true value of what we're building here. I'm asking you to look beyond the short-term gain and see the incredible future we're creating."

As Bob finished speaking, the room fell silent. He could see the board members exchanging glances, some thoughtful, some skeptical. The chairman leaned forward, his expression unreadable.

"Thank you, Bob," he said. "You've given us a lot to think about. We'll need some time to deliberate."

The next few hours were among the longest of Bob's life. He paced the halls of Maple and Brick, trying to distract himself by checking in on various projects, but his mind kept returning to the board room and the decision being made there.

Finally, as the sun was setting, painting the old maple tree outside in hues of gold and red, Bob received the call he had been waiting for. The board had reached a decision.

With his heart pounding, Bob returned to the board room. The chairman stood as he entered, a small smile playing on his lips.

"Bob," he began, "I want to thank you for your passionate and compelling presentation. After much discussion, the board has decided to reject the acquisition offers and fully commit to continuing Maple and Brick's transformation journey."

Bob felt a wave of relief and joy wash over him. They had done it. They had secured the future of Maple and Brick as an independent, innovative force in American manufacturing.

As he left the board room and walked through the factory, sharing the good news with his team, Bob felt a renewed sense of purpose and determination. They had faced trials and tribulations, they had been tested in ways they never expected, but they had emerged stronger for it.

The journey of transformation was far from over. There would be more challenges to face, more obstacles to overcome. But now, Bob knew with certainty that Maple and Brick was on the right path. They were not just adapting to the future – they were actively shaping it.

As the lights of the factory glowed warmly in the gathering dusk, Bob paused for a moment beneath the old maple tree. He placed his hand on its rough bark, feeling a connection to all those who had stood in this spot before him, facing their own trials and tribulations.

"We're still here," he murmured. "Still growing, still innovating. The legacy lives on."

With that, Bob turned and walked back into the factory, ready to lead Maple and Brick into the next chapter of its remarkable story. The trials they had faced had only made them stronger, more resilient, and more committed to their vision of a bright and innovative future. And in that strength lay the promise of great things to come.

CHAPTER 13 REFLECTION: TRIALS AND TRIBULATIONS

Key Insights:
- ❖ True transformation is tested through trials and tribulations.
- ❖ Overcoming challenges refines strategy and strengthens resolve.

Personal Reflection:

Think about a time when your commitment to a goal was severely tested. How did you overcome the challenges you faced? What did these trials teach you about yourself and your mission?

Application Question:

How can you use the lessons learned from past trials to better prepare for and navigate future challenges in your transformative journey?

Action Step:

Conduct a "trial analysis" of your current project or goal. Identify potential obstacles and create contingency plans for each, drawing on your past experiences of overcoming challenges.

Quote to Remember:

"It is through the fires of trial that our vision is refined and our determination is forged."

CHAPTER 14: THE TOWN'S AWAKENING

The first light of dawn painted the sky in soft hues of pink and gold as Bob Harrington drove through the quiet streets of Peterborough. The town was just beginning to stir, shopkeepers sweeping their storefronts, early risers jogging along the sidewalks. As he passed the town square, Bob's eyes were drawn to a new banner hanging from the town hall: "Peterborough Innovation Week: Embracing the Future, Honoring Our Past."

A smile tugged at Bob's lips. The transformation of Maple and Brick had sparked something in the town, a rekindling of the innovative spirit that had once made Peterborough a hub of industry and creativity. The upcoming Innovation Week was a testament to that awakening.

As Bob pulled into the Maple and Brick parking lot, he noticed a group of high school students being led into the factory by Emily. The sight filled him with pride; their new educational outreach program was just one of the ways they were working to integrate the company more deeply into the fabric of the community.

Inside, the factory was abuzz with activity. In addition to the regular production work, various areas had been set up to showcase Maple and Brick's innovations to the town during the upcoming week. Bob made his way through the controlled chaos, stopping to chat with employees and check on the progress of different exhibits.

He found Joe in the advanced manufacturing area, carefully adjusting a display that showed the evolution of their production techniques. The old machinist's face lit up as he saw Bob approach.

"Morning, Mr. Harrington," Joe called out. "Just putting the finishing touches on our exhibit. Can you believe it? People used to think of us as just another old factory, and now we're leading the charge into the future of manufacturing."

Bob nodded, feeling a swell of pride. "It's remarkable, isn't it? And it's not just us. Have you seen what's happening in town?"

Joe's eyes twinkled. "Oh, I've seen it alright. My grandson's school is starting a robotics club, inspired by our work here. And I heard the old textile mill down by the river is being converted into a tech incubator for local startups."

As they continued to chat, Alex approached, a tablet in hand and an excited gleam in her eye. "Bob, you need to see this," she said, handing him the device. "It's the latest economic report for Peterborough."

Bob scrolled through the document, his eyes widening as he took in the figures. New business registrations were up 30% year over year. The town's unemployment rate had dropped to its lowest level in two decades. Property values were rising, but not at a rate that was pricing out long-time residents.

"This is incredible," Bob murmured. "I knew our efforts were having an impact on the town, but I had no idea it was to this extent."

Alex nodded, her face beaming. "It's not just the direct impact of our operations. The spirit of innovation we've fostered is spreading. Other businesses in town are following our lead, modernizing their operations, exploring new markets. And we're attracting talent from all over the region."

Their conversation was interrupted by the arrival of Laura, who was practically bouncing with excitement. "Bob, Alex, you won't believe who just confirmed for our Innovation Week keynote address," she said, pausing for dramatic effect. "Dr. Evelyn Turner herself!"

Bob felt a jolt of surprise and pleasure. Dr. Turner, their original transformation consultant, had gone on to become a leading figure in the field of organizational innovation. Her willingness to return to Peterborough was a powerful endorsement of what they had achieved.

As the day progressed, Bob found himself constantly amazed by the energy and enthusiasm he saw, not just within Maple and Brick, but throughout the town. He attended a meeting at the Chamber of Commerce, where local business leaders eagerly discussed plans for collaborative innovation initiatives. He visited the high school, where students proudly showed off projects they had developed as part of a new STEM program sponsored by Maple and Brick.

By late afternoon, Bob found himself standing in the town square, taking in the transformation around him. The once-sleepy main street now bustled with activity. A new co-working space had opened in a formerly vacant storefront, its windows plastered with flyers for tech meetups and entrepreneurship workshops. The old diner where he had eaten countless meals over the years now boasted a sign advertising "locally sourced, sustainably produced ingredients."

As he stood there, lost in thought, he felt a hand on his shoulder. It was Sarah Mitchell, the town's mayor, her face wreathed in a warm smile.

"Quite a change, isn't it?" she said, gesturing to the vibrant scene around them. "You know, when you first started talking about transforming Maple and Brick, some folks in town were skeptical. They worried you'd automate everything and cut jobs, or worse, shut down and move operations overseas."

Bob nodded, remembering those tense early days. "And now?"

Sarah's smile widened. "Now, you're the town's biggest cheerleader. The way you've integrated Maple and Brick into the community, the opportunities you're creating, the spirit of innovation you're fostering... it's woken something up in Peterborough. People are excited about the future again."

As they continued to chat, Bob's attention was drawn to a group of young people gathered around a 3D printer set up in the square. They were part of a new youth entrepreneurship program, excitedly discussing ideas for products they could design and prototype.

"You see that?" Sarah said, following Bob's gaze. "That's the future of Peterborough right there. And it's happening because you showed us all what's possible when you embrace change while honoring your roots."

The next few days leading up to Innovation Week were a whirlwind of activity. Maple and Brick was at the center of it all, hosting tours, conducting workshops, and showcasing their latest innovations. But they were far from alone. Local businesses, schools, and community organizations had all gotten into the spirit, organizing their own events and exhibits.

The week kicked off with a town-wide parade, celebrating Peterborough's history of innovation and its bright future. Bob watched with a lump in his throat as floats depicting the town's past achievements in textiles and manufacturing gave way to showcases of cutting-edge technology and sustainable design.

Throughout the week, the energy in the town was palpable. Visitors poured in from all over the region, eager to see what Peterborough had become. Local bed and breakfasts were fully booked, restaurants were packed, and the streets buzzed with excited conversation.

At Maple and Brick, every day brought new wonders. Emily's team conducted live demonstrations of their latest sustainable materials, drawing gasps of amazement from onlookers as they showed off the strength and versatility of their nanoparticle-enhanced polymers. Joe and the production team led tours of the advanced manufacturing floor, proudly explaining how they had blended traditional craftsmanship with cutting-edge technology.

One of the highlights came midweek, when a group of students from the local high school presented a project they had developed in collaboration with Maple and Brick engineers – a solar-powered water purification system designed for use in developing countries. The pride on the students' faces as they explained their invention was matched only by the pride Bob felt in seeing how Maple and Brick's transformation had inspired the next generation.

As the week neared its end, anticipation built for Dr. Evelyn Turner's keynote address. The event was held in the town hall, which was packed to capacity with locals and visitors alike. As Bob introduced Dr. Turner, he couldn't help but reflect on how far they had come since she had first arrived in Peterborough to guide their transformation.

Dr. Turner's speech was a tour de force, weaving together the story of Maple and Brick's transformation with broader trends in innovation and community development. She praised Peterborough for embracing change while staying true to its values, holding it up as a model for other small towns facing economic challenges.

"What you've achieved here is remarkable," Dr. Turner concluded, her voice ringing through the hall. "You've shown that innovation isn't just about technology or profit. It's about people, community, and the courage to reimagine what's possible. Peterborough isn't just adapting to the future – it's helping to shape it."

As the crowd rose in a standing ovation, Bob felt a wave of emotion wash over him. This was so much bigger than just Maple and Brick now. They had sparked a transformation that had revitalized an entire community.

The final day of Innovation Week dawned clear and bright. As Bob walked through the town, he was struck by the sense of possibility that seemed to hang in the air. Everywhere he looked, he saw signs of renewal and growth – new businesses opening, old buildings being renovated, people of all ages engaged in excited discussion about future projects and opportunities.

As he reached the town square, he found Alex waiting for him, a knowing smile on her face. "So," she said, "what do you think? Has Peterborough embraced innovation?"

Bob laughed, gesturing to the vibrant scene around them. "I'd say that's an understatement. This town... it's come alive in a way I never could have imagined."

Alex nodded, her expression turning thoughtful. "You know, when we started this journey, we were focused on transforming Maple and Brick. But what you've done here goes so far beyond that. You've shown that when a company truly integrates itself into its community, when it leads by example and inspires others to innovate, the impact can be transformative on a much larger scale."

As they stood there, watching the town buzzing with activity, Bob felt a profound sense of pride and purpose. The awakening of Peterborough was more than just an economic revitalization. It was a rebirth of spirit, a renewed belief in the power of innovation and community to create a better future.

The transformation journey was far from over. There would be new challenges to face, new opportunities to seize. But now, Maple and Brick wasn't facing them alone. They were part of a vibrant, innovative ecosystem, a community united in its commitment to embracing the future while honoring its past.

As the sun climbed higher in the sky, painting the town in warm, golden light, Bob Harrington smiled. The legacy of Maple and Brick had grown beyond the factory walls. It now lived in the hearts and minds of an entire town, awakened to the possibilities of innovation and ready to write the next chapter in its storied history.

The journey continued, and Peterborough was wide awake, ready to face whatever the future might bring.

CHAPTER 14 REFLECTION: THE TOWN'S AWAKENING

Key Insights:

- ❖ Transformation is not just an internal process; it impacts and inspires the broader community.
- ❖ Positive change can create a ripple effect, awakening potential in unexpected places.

Personal Reflection:

Consider a time when your actions or decisions had a wider impact than you initially anticipated. How did this ripple effect manifest, and what did it teach you about the interconnectedness of change?

Application Question:

How can you ensure that your personal or organizational transformation benefits and inspires those around you? What opportunities exist to engage your broader community in your journey?

Action Step:

Identify one way you can share the lessons or benefits of your transformation with your wider community. Plan an event, write a blog post, or initiate a conversation to spread the impact of your journey.

Quote to Remember:

"True transformation echoes far beyond ourselves, awakening possibility in the hearts of others."

CHAPTER 15: A NEW VISION EMERGES

The soft glow of dawn was just beginning to paint the sky as Bob Harrington stood atop the highest hill in Peterborough, looking down at the town sprawled below. The transformation of Maple and Brick had sparked a renaissance in Peterborough, and from this vantage point, Bob could see the physical manifestations of that change.

The old textile mill, once a relic of the town's industrial past, now gleamed with new purpose as a thriving tech incubator. The main street, which had been dotted with vacant storefronts just a few years ago, now bustled with activity, a mix of innovative startups and revitalized traditional businesses. And there, at the heart of it all, stood Maple and Brick, its brick facade a testament to its enduring legacy, even as it led the charge into the future.

As Bob absorbed the view, he felt a presence beside him. It was Alex, who had become not just a consultant but a true partner in their journey of transformation.

"It's quite a sight, isn't it?" Alex said, her voice soft with wonder.

Bob nodded, a lump forming in his throat. "Sometimes I can hardly believe how far we've come. But Alex, I can't shake the feeling that we're on the cusp of something even bigger."

Alex turned to him, her eyes bright with curiosity. "What do you mean?"

Bob took a deep breath, organizing his thoughts. "We've transformed Maple and Brick. We've helped revitalize Peterborough. But what if that's just the beginning? What if we could take what we've learned here and use it to make a difference on an even larger scale?"

As they made their way down the hill and towards the factory, Bob shared the vision that had been forming in his mind. He spoke of creating a network of innovation hubs across small towns in America, each one building on the model they had developed at Maple and Brick. He envisioned a future where traditional manufacturing and cutting-edge technology worked hand in hand, where small towns could once again become engines of economic growth and innovation.

By the time they reached Maple and Brick, the early shift was already arriving. Bob and Alex made their way to the conference room, where the core team was gathering for their weekly strategy meeting. As they entered, Bob could feel the energy in the room – a mix of excitement and anticipation that had become the norm since their transformation began.

"Good morning, everyone," Bob began, his voice filled with an enthusiasm that immediately caught everyone's attention. "Before we dive into our regular agenda, I want to share something with you. A vision that I believe could be the next chapter in Maple and Brick's story."

Over the next hour, Bob laid out his idea. He spoke of the impact they had made in Peterborough and how they could potentially replicate and expand that impact across the country. He outlined a plan to establish a network of innovation centers, each one tailored to the unique strengths and needs of its community, but all connected by a shared commitment to blending traditional craftsmanship with cutting-edge technology.

As he spoke, Bob could see the idea taking hold in the minds of his team. Emily's eyes lit up as she considered the potential for spreading their sustainable manufacturing techniques. Joe, who had once been the most resistant to change, now leaned forward eagerly, no doubt thinking of how his expertise could be shared with a new generation of craftsmen across the country.

Laura was already scribbling notes, her marketing mind spinning with the possibilities. "This isn't just about expanding our business," she said, looking up from her notepad. "This is about redefining the narrative around American manufacturing. We could change the way people think about small towns and traditional industries."

Jacob chimed in, his voice filled with excitement. "And think about the technological possibilities. We could create a network of interconnected smart factories, sharing data and innovations in real-time. The potential for collaborative problem-solving and rapid innovation is enormous."

As the discussion continued, the energy in the room built to a palpable crescendo. Ideas flew back and forth, each one building on the last, as the team began to flesh out the details of this ambitious new vision.

Alex, who had been quietly observing, finally spoke up. "This is incredibly exciting," she said, her voice measured but unable to hide her enthusiasm. "But it's also a massive undertaking. We need to consider the challenges carefully."

She began to outline the potential obstacles: the need for significant capital investment, the challenge of scaling their model while maintaining its integrity, the potential resistance from communities wary of outside influence.

But for every challenge Alex raised, the team had a potential solution. They spoke of partnering with local investors and community leaders in each town, of developing a flexible model that could adapt to each community's unique circumstances, of leveraging their success in Peterborough as a proof of concept to win over skeptics.

As the meeting wound down, Bob felt a sense of awe at the collective wisdom and creativity of his team. What had started as a vague idea in his mind had been transformed, through the crucible of their combined expertise and imagination, into a bold, actionable vision for the future.

"Alright," Bob said, bringing the discussion to a close. "We've got a lot of work ahead of us to turn this vision into reality. But I believe we've got the right team to do it. Let's take the next week to refine these ideas, do some initial research, and then we'll reconvene to start putting together a concrete plan."

As the team filed out, energized and chattering excitedly about the possibilities, Bob turned to Alex. "Well," he said, a mix of excitement and trepidation in his voice, "what do you think? Are we crazy for even considering this?"

Alex smiled, her eyes twinkling. "Oh, it's definitely crazy," she said. "But the best innovations always are. And if anyone can pull this off, it's this team."

Over the next few weeks, Maple and Brick was abuzz with activity as they worked to develop their ambitious new vision. Every department was involved, bringing their unique perspectives and expertise to the table.

Emily and her R&D team began exploring how their sustainable manufacturing techniques could be adapted to different industries and environments. Joe worked with the production team to develop training programs that could effectively transmit their blend of traditional craftsmanship and high-tech manufacturing to workers in other communities.

Laura and her marketing team started crafting a narrative around the project, positioning Maple and Brick not just as a company, but as the spark for a new American manufacturing renaissance. Jacob and the IT department began designing the technological infrastructure that would connect the proposed network of innovation hubs.

As the plan began to take shape, Bob knew it was time to bring in outside perspectives. He organized a series of town halls, inviting community leaders, educators, and residents to share their thoughts on the proposal. The response was overwhelmingly positive, with many seeing the potential for Peterborough to become a model for small-town revitalization across the country.

One evening, as Bob was leaving one of these community meetings, he was approached by an elderly woman. She introduced herself as Margaret, a lifelong resident of Peterborough.

"You know," she said, her eyes misty with emotion, "I've seen this town go through a lot of changes over the years. There were times when I thought our best days were behind us. But what you're doing, what you're planning... it gives me hope. Hope for Peterborough, and hope for all the other small towns out there facing the same challenges we did."

Her words stayed with Bob, reinforcing his commitment to seeing this vision through. This wasn't just about business growth or technological innovation. It was about preserving and revitalizing communities, about giving people hope for the future.

As the weeks turned into months, the vision continued to evolve and solidify. They brought in experts in urban planning, economic development, and social entrepreneurship to help refine their approach. They began identifying potential partner communities, looking for places with a strong manufacturing heritage and a willingness to embrace innovation.

The board, initially skeptical of such an ambitious plan, gradually came around as they saw the potential for long-term growth and the positive impact on Maple and Brick's brand. They approved an initial budget for pilot programs in three communities, with the potential for further expansion based on the results.

Finally, after months of planning and preparation, Bob stood before his team, ready to officially launch their new initiative. The conference room was packed, with every employee who could be spared from their duties in attendance. The atmosphere was electric with anticipation.

"Ladies and gentlemen," Bob began, his voice strong and clear, "today marks the beginning of a new chapter, not just for Maple and Brick, but for American manufacturing as a whole. We call it the 'Revive and Thrive Initiative'."

He went on to outline their vision: a network of innovation hubs across small-town America, each one building on the model they had developed in Peterborough. These hubs would blend traditional manufacturing with cutting-edge technology, creating jobs, spurring innovation, and revitalizing communities.

"We're not just expanding our business," Bob continued, his voice filled with passion. "We're exporting hope. We're showing that small towns can be at the forefront of innovation, that traditional industries can be reimagined for the 21st century, that American manufacturing isn't just alive – it's evolving and thriving."

As Bob concluded his speech, the room erupted in applause. He could see the excitement on every face, the shared sense of purpose that had become the hallmark of Maple and Brick's culture.

Later that day, as the sun began to set, Bob found himself once again standing beneath the old maple tree outside the factory. He placed his hand on its rough bark, feeling a connection to all those who had stood in this spot before him, facing their own challenges and dreaming their own big dreams.

"Well, old girl," he said softly, "looks like we're about to embark on our biggest adventure yet. But no matter how far we go, no matter how much we grow, this will always be home. This will always be where it all began."

As he turned to head back into the factory, Bob felt a profound sense of excitement and purpose. A new vision had emerged, one that would carry Maple and Brick – and hopefully, countless other communities – into a bright and innovative future.

The transformation journey continued, but now it was no longer just about one company or one town. It was about reimagining the very fabric of American manufacturing and small-town life. And as Bob Harrington stepped back into the bustling factory, he knew that the best was yet to come.

CHAPTER 15 REFLECTION: A NEW VISION EMERGES

Key Insights:
- ❖ A clear, compelling vision is the compass that guides successful transformation.
- ❖ As the vision becomes clearer, the path forward gains momentum and purpose.

Personal Reflection:

Reflect on how your vision for the future has evolved throughout your transformative journey. How has this evolving vision influenced your actions and decisions?

Application Question:

How can you further clarify and effectively communicate your vision to inspire and align others in your transformation efforts?

Action Step:

Create a vision board or written statement that captures your emerging vision. Share it with key stakeholders and gather their input to refine and strengthen it.

Quote to Remember:

"A powerful vision does not just predict the future – it creates it."

CHAPTER 16: TRANSFORMATION IN ACTION

The early morning mist clung to the ground as Bob Harrington's car wound its way through the rolling hills of rural Pennsylvania. It had been six months since Maple and Brick had launched their ambitious "Revive and Thrive Initiative," and today marked a significant milestone. They were about to break ground on their first innovation hub outside of Peterborough.

As Bob crested a hill, the town of Millbrook came into view. Like so many small American towns, Millbrook had fallen on hard times in recent decades. Its once-thriving furniture manufacturing industry had all but disappeared, leaving behind empty factories and a struggling community.

But today, there was an energy in the air that hadn't been felt in Millbrook for years. As Bob pulled into the town square, he saw banners proclaiming "Welcome Maple and Brick" and "A New Era for Millbrook." A crowd had already begun to gather near the old Hartley Furniture factory, which would soon be transformed into Millbrook's innovation hub.

Bob spotted Alex Chen standing near the podium that had been set up for the groundbreaking ceremony. As he approached, he could see the mixture of excitement and apprehension in her eyes.

"Morning, Bob," Alex greeted him. "Are you ready for this?"

Bob took a deep breath, looking out over the growing crowd. "As ready as I'll ever be. This is it, Alex. This is where we prove that our vision can work beyond Peterborough."

As they chatted, Bob saw familiar faces from his team mingling with the locals. Emily was deep in conversation with a group that included Millbrook's mayor and several former furniture workers, no doubt discussing how traditional woodworking skills could be blended with new sustainable materials and technologies. Joe was showing a group of young people around a mobile manufacturing unit they had brought as a demonstration, his gruff voice carrying over the crowd as he explained how modern tech could enhance traditional craftsmanship.

At 9 AM sharp, Millbrook's mayor, Sandra Thompson, stepped up to the podium to begin the ceremony. "Ladies and gentlemen," she began, her voice ringing out over the assembled crowd, "today marks a new chapter in Millbrook's history. For too long, we've been a town living in the shadow of our past glory. But thanks to the vision of Maple and Brick and the 'Revive and Thrive Initiative,' we have the opportunity to write a new story – a story of innovation, of renewal, of hope."

As Mayor Thompson continued her speech, Bob found his mind wandering to the journey that had brought them to this moment. The challenges they had faced in Peterborough, the lessons they had learned, the risks they had taken – all of it had led to this. They were no longer just transforming a single company or town; they were embarking on a mission to reshape the landscape of American manufacturing.

When it was Bob's turn to speak, he stepped up to the podium, feeling the weight of expectation from both the Millbrook residents and his own team. "Thank you, Mayor Thompson, and thank you to everyone in Millbrook for your warm welcome and your faith in this vision," he began.

"What we're starting here today is more than just a new business venture. It's a partnership between Maple and Brick and the people of Millbrook. We're not here to replace your rich manufacturing heritage, but to help it evolve and thrive in the 21st century."

Bob went on to outline their plans for the innovation hub – how it would combine advanced manufacturing technologies with traditional craftsmanship, how it would provide training programs to help workers adapt to new technologies, and how it would serve as an incubator for local entrepreneurs looking to start their own innovative businesses.

"But most importantly," Bob concluded, "we're here to learn from you. The spirit of innovation that built Millbrook's furniture industry is still alive in this community. Together, we're going to show the world that small-town America isn't just surviving – it's innovating, it's growing, it's thriving."

As Bob finished his speech to enthusiastic applause, he couldn't help but feel a sense of déjà vu. It reminded him of the early days of Maple and Brick's transformation, that mixture of excitement and uncertainty, of hope tinged with the knowledge of the hard work ahead.

The groundbreaking itself was a symbolic affair, with Bob, Mayor Thompson, and several community leaders turning over shovelfuls of earth where the new addition to the old factory would be built. But as soon as the ceremony was over, the real work began.

Teams from Maple and Brick, working alongside local contractors and former factory workers, swarmed over the old Hartley Furniture building. The plan was to preserve as much of the original structure as possible, honoring its history while retrofitting it with the latest in sustainable and smart building technologies.

Over the next few weeks, Bob split his time between Peterborough and Millbrook, overseeing the progress of the new hub while ensuring that Maple and Brick's core operations continued to run smoothly. It was a grueling schedule, but the energy and excitement of the project kept him going.

One afternoon, about a month into the renovation, Bob was walking through the partially completed hub with Joe and a group of former Hartley Furniture workers. They were discussing how to integrate some of the old woodworking machinery with new computer-controlled systems.

"The key," Joe was saying, his hands gesturing animatedly, "is to use the technology to enhance the craftsmanship, not replace it. These old machines, they've got a feel to them that you can't replicate with purely automated systems. But if we can use the computers to handle the precision cuts and the repetitive tasks, it frees up the craftsmen to focus on the details that really make a piece special."

Bob watched with pride as Joe worked with the local craftsmen, bridging the gap between old and new. It was a perfect encapsulation of what they were trying to achieve with the "Revive and Thrive Initiative" – honoring traditional skills while embracing new technologies.

As the hub began to take shape, so too did the community's engagement with the project. Emily had set up a series of workshops and classes, teaching everything from 3D modeling for furniture design to the properties of new sustainable materials. To everyone's surprise, these classes were soon oversubscribed, with attendees ranging from former factory workers to high school students.

Laura and her team had been hard at work as well, not just promoting the Millbrook hub but using it to tell a larger story about the revitalization of small-town manufacturing. They had invited journalists from major publications to tour the facility, resulting in a series of articles that caught national attention.

One piece in a prominent business magazine described the Millbrook hub as "a blueprint for the future of American manufacturing," praising the way it blended traditional skills with cutting-edge technology. Another, in a major newspaper, focused on the human story, profiling several Millbrook residents whose lives had been transformed by the opportunities the hub provided.

The growing national attention brought both opportunities and challenges. Inquiries began pouring in from other small towns across the country, all eager to be considered for future innovation hubs. While this validated their vision, it also put pressure on Bob and his team to deliver results in Millbrook before expanding further.

There were setbacks too. Some of the integration between old and new technologies proved more challenging than anticipated, leading to delays and cost overruns. A few of the older workers struggled to adapt to the new systems, leading to frustration and some heated discussions about the pace of change.

But for every challenge, there seemed to be a breakthrough. A group of young entrepreneurs, inspired by the hub's 3D printing capabilities, started a company creating custom furniture components that quickly gained traction in the high-end design market. A collaboration between Millbrook's traditional woodworkers and Maple and Brick's materials scientists led to the development of a new type of engineered wood that was stronger, more sustainable, and uniquely beautiful.

Six months after the groundbreaking, the Millbrook Innovation Hub was ready for its official opening. The transformation was stunning. The old Hartley Furniture factory, once a symbol of the town's decline, now gleamed with a mix of restored brick and sleek modern additions. Solar panels on the roof and a small wind turbine nearby showcased its commitment to sustainability.

Inside, the hub hummed with activity. In one area, skilled craftsmen worked with computer-aided design tools to create intricate furniture pieces. In another, a group of students learned to program and operate advanced CNC machines. The incubator space was already home to several promising startups, their energy and enthusiasm palpable.

As Bob prepared to cut the ribbon for the official opening ceremony, he found himself reflecting on the journey that had brought them to this point. The transformation of Maple and Brick had been just the beginning. Here in Millbrook, they were seeing their vision come to life on a larger scale.

"Ladies and gentlemen," Bob began, addressing the large crowd gathered for the opening, "what we're celebrating today is more than just the opening of a new facility. We're celebrating a new chapter in the story of American manufacturing. A chapter that honors our past while boldly embracing the future."

He went on to highlight some of the hub's early successes – the jobs created, the new businesses launched, the innovations already emerging from the collaboration between traditional skills and new technologies.

"But this is just the beginning," Bob continued, his voice filled with passion. "What we've started here in Millbrook, what we're continuing in Peterborough, this is a model for revitalization that can be replicated across the country. We're proving that with the right blend of innovation, community engagement, and respect for traditional skills, small-town America can once again be at the forefront of manufacturing and innovation."

As Bob cut the ribbon, officially opening the Millbrook Innovation Hub, the crowd erupted in cheers. He could see tears in the eyes of some of the older residents, people who had watched their town struggle for decades and were now witnessing its rebirth.

In the days that followed the opening, Bob found himself fielding calls from investors, politicians, and community leaders from across the country, all interested in bringing the "Revive and Thrive Initiative" to their own communities. The success in Millbrook had turned what was once a bold vision into a proven concept, opening doors and creating opportunities they had only dreamed of months before.

But even as he looked to the future and the potential for further expansion, Bob never lost sight of the human element at the heart of their mission. He thought of Debbie, a former Hartley Furniture worker in her 50s who had become one of the hub's most enthusiastic adopters of new technology, now leading workshops for other workers transitioning to the new systems. He thought of Mike, a young entrepreneur whose sustainable furniture startup, incubated at the hub, was already attracting national attention.

These stories, and countless others like them, were the true measure of their success. They were transforming not just industries or economies, but people's lives and communities.

As Bob prepared to return to Peterborough, he took one last walk through the Millbrook hub. The place was alive with activity – the whir of machinery, the tap of keyboards, the animated discussions of people engaged in creative problem-solving. This, he realized, was transformation in action. Not just a concept or a plan, but a living, breathing reality.

The journey was far from over. There would be new challenges to face, new problems to solve, new opportunities to seize. But as Bob looked out over the bustling hub, he felt a profound sense of purpose and optimism. They were not just adapting to the future of manufacturing; they were actively shaping it. And in doing so, they were breathing new life into the heart of America, one small town at a time.

The transformation continued, and its ripples were spreading far beyond what they had ever imagined. As Bob stepped out into the Millbrook sunshine, he knew that the best was yet to come. The future of American manufacturing was being written, not in sprawling urban centers, but in small towns like Millbrook and Peterborough, where innovation and tradition were coming together to create something truly remarkable.

CHAPTER 16 REFLECTION: TRANSFORMATION IN ACTION

Key Insights:

- ❖ Transformation becomes tangible when it moves from theory to action.
- ❖ Seeing the results of your efforts fuels further innovation and growth.

Personal Reflection:

Think about a moment when you saw the tangible results of your transformation efforts. How did this impact your motivation and commitment to the journey?

Application Question:

How can you better measure and celebrate the small wins along your transformation journey? How might this practice sustain momentum and inspire continued effort?

Action Step:

Implement a system to track and celebrate progress in your transformation journey. This could be a weekly review, a visual progress chart, or regular team celebrations of milestones achieved.

Quote to Remember:

"Transformation is not just about grand visions, but about the daily actions that bring those visions to life."

CHAPTER 17:
THE FINAL TEST

The autumn wind whipped through the streets of Peterborough, sending leaves swirling in intricate dances as Bob Harrington made his way to Maple and Brick. The company had been riding a wave of success following the triumphant launch of the Millbrook Innovation Hub, but as Bob approached the factory, he couldn't shake a feeling of unease.

His instincts proved correct as he entered the building to find Alex waiting for him, her face etched with concern. "Bob, we need to talk," she said, her tone grave. "There's been a development."

In the privacy of Bob's office, Alex laid out the situation. A major tech conglomerate, Global Innovations Inc., had announced plans to launch a series of "smart manufacturing centers" across the country. Their model bore a striking resemblance to Maple and Brick's "Revive and Thrive Initiative," but with the backing of billions in corporate capital.

"They're moving fast," Alex explained, pulling up a map on her tablet. "They've already broken ground on three sites, and they're in talks with at least a dozen more communities."

Bob felt his stomach drop. This was exactly the kind of competition they had feared – a corporate giant with deep pockets and a vast network of resources. "How did we not see this coming?" he muttered, more to himself than to Alex.

"We've been so focused on our own growth, on making sure Millbrook succeeded, that we might have missed the bigger picture," Alex admitted. "But that's not the worst of it."

She hesitated for a moment before continuing. "They've made an offer to acquire Maple and Brick. The board is considering it."

The news hit Bob like a physical blow. Everything they had worked for, the culture they had built, the vision they had for revitalizing small-town America – it could all be swallowed up by a faceless corporation.

As the core team gathered for an emergency meeting, the mood was somber. Laura from marketing was the first to speak up. "We need to get ahead of this," she insisted. "If we can show the board and the public that our model is superior, that we're not just about profits but about genuine community revitalization, we might have a chance."

Emily nodded in agreement. "Our innovation pipeline is strong. We've got projects in development that could revolutionize sustainable manufacturing. If we can accelerate some of these, showcase what sets us apart..."

Joe, who had been uncharacteristically quiet, finally spoke up. "It's not just about the technology," he said, his voice gruff with emotion. "What we've built here, in Peterborough and Millbrook, it's about people. It's about community. No corporate giant can replicate that overnight."

As the discussion continued, Bob found his mind racing. They needed to act fast, to prove beyond a shadow of a doubt that Maple and Brick's approach was unique and valuable. But how?

It was Jacob who provided the spark of inspiration. "What if we open-source some of our technologies?" he suggested. "Not everything, of course, but enough to show that we're committed to more than just our own bottom line. We could create a network of independent innovation hubs, all working together to drive American manufacturing forward."

The idea took hold, and soon the room was buzzing with energy as the team began to flesh out a plan. They would accelerate their most promising innovations, open-source key technologies, and launch a massive outreach campaign to showcase the real, human impact of their work.

Over the next few weeks, Maple and Brick entered a state of controlled chaos. Every department was working overtime, pushing the boundaries of what they thought possible.

Emily and her R&D team made a breakthrough in their work on self-healing materials, creating a prototype that could revolutionize everything from consumer electronics to aerospace components. Joe and the production team streamlined their hybrid manufacturing process, achieving levels of efficiency and quality that surpassed even their most optimistic projections.

Laura and her marketing team worked tirelessly to tell Maple and Brick's story, not just through traditional media, but through a series of powerful documentaries showcasing the transformation of Peterborough and Millbrook. They highlighted not just the economic impact, but the renewed sense of pride and purpose in these communities.

Jacob led the charge on the open-source initiative, carefully selecting technologies that could be shared without compromising Maple and Brick's competitive edge. The response from the maker community and small-scale manufacturers was overwhelming, with a flood of innovations and improvements flowing back to Maple and Brick.

But perhaps the most powerful response came from the communities themselves. When word spread about the potential corporate takeover, Peterborough and Millbrook rallied around Maple and Brick. Local businesses put up signs supporting the company, schools organized letter-writing campaigns to the board, and town halls were packed with residents eager to share how Maple and Brick had changed their lives.

As the date of the board's decision approached, Bob found himself working around the clock, coordinating efforts, making pitches to key stakeholders, and trying to keep his team's morale high. The strain was beginning to show, not just on him, but on everyone at Maple and Brick.

The night before the board meeting, Bob found himself once again standing beneath the old maple tree outside the factory. He placed his hand on its gnarled trunk, feeling a connection to all those who had stood in this spot before him, facing their own trials and tribulations.

"We've come too far to give up now," he murmured, as much to himself as to the tree. "This isn't just about a company. It's about a vision for the future of American manufacturing, for the revitalization of small-town America."

As he turned to head back into the factory for one last strategy session, Bob saw a group of employees gathered near the entrance. To his surprise, they began to applaud as he approached. It was a small gesture, but in that moment, it meant everything.

The next morning, as Bob prepared to make his final pitch to the board, he felt a calm determination settle over him. They had done everything they could. Now, it was time to make their case.

The board room was packed, not just with board members, but with representatives from Global Innovations Inc., local officials, and key employees from Maple and Brick. Bob took a deep breath and began his presentation.

He spoke of the journey Maple and Brick had undertaken, from a struggling traditional manufacturer to a beacon of innovation. He showcased their technological breakthroughs, their commitment to sustainability, and their open-source initiatives. But most importantly, he talked about the impact they had made on real people and real communities.

"What we've built at Maple and Brick isn't just a business model," Bob said, his voice filled with passion. "It's a movement. A movement to revitalize American manufacturing, to breathe new life into small towns, to prove that we can innovate and compete on a global scale while still staying true to our values."

As Bob concluded his presentation, the room fell silent. He could see the board members exchanging glances, their expressions unreadable.

The Final Test

The representative from Global Innovations Inc. leaned forward, about to speak, when suddenly the doors burst open.

To everyone's surprise, a group of people from Peterborough and Millbrook filed into the room. There was Mary, the former textile worker who now led advanced manufacturing training programs. Mike, the young entrepreneur whose sustainable furniture startup had taken off. Mayor Thompson from Millbrook, and dozens of others whose lives had been transformed by Maple and Brick's initiatives.

One by one, they stepped forward to share their stories. They spoke of renewed hope, of children returning to towns they had once fled, of a sense of pride and purpose that had been lost and was now found again.

As the last person finished speaking, Bob looked around the room. He could see tears in the eyes of several board members. Even the Global Innovations representative looked moved.

The board chairman cleared his throat. "I think," he said, his voice thick with emotion, "that we've heard everything we need to hear. There will be no sale. Maple and Brick will remain independent, free to continue its mission."

The room erupted in cheers. Bob felt a wave of relief and joy wash over him. They had done it. They had faced their final test and emerged stronger than ever.

In the days that followed, the impact of the board's decision rippled out far beyond Maple and Brick. Their story had captured the national imagination, sparking conversations about the future of manufacturing, the revitalization of small-town America, and the power of innovation rooted in community.

Global Innovations Inc., in a surprising move, reached out to discuss a partnership rather than a takeover. Other companies and communities across the country began to adopt elements of Maple and Brick's model, creating a network of independent but interconnected innovation hubs.

As Bob stood on the factory floor, watching the hum of activity around him, he felt a profound sense of pride and purpose. They had not just saved a company; they had sparked a movement. The transformation that had begun in one struggling factory had grown into something far greater than they had ever imagined.

The journey wasn't over – in many ways, it was just beginning. But now, Maple and Brick was ready to lead the way into a new era of American manufacturing, one that balanced innovation with tradition, profit with purpose, and corporate success with community revitalization.

As the sun set on another day of innovation and possibility, Bob smiled to himself. They had faced their final test, and in doing so, had opened the door to a future brighter than they had ever dared to dream.

CHAPTER 17 REFLECTION: THE FINAL TEST

Key Insights:
- ❖ Every transformation faces a decisive moment that determines its success or failure.
- ❖ This final test often demands everything learned throughout the journey.

Personal Reflection:
Recall a time when you faced a critical, make-or-break moment in a project or personal endeavor. How did you prepare for and navigate this challenge?

Application Question:
How can you prepare yourself and your team for the ultimate test of your transformation efforts? What resources, skills, or mindsets might you need to cultivate?

Action Step:
Conduct a "final test" simulation. Identify potential critical challenges and run through scenarios to practice your response and refine your strategies.

Quote to Remember:
"The final test of transformation is not just a measure of our work, but of our growth."

CHAPTER 18: REBIRTH AND LEGACY

The warm spring breeze carried the scent of new beginnings as Bob Harrington stood beneath the old maple tree outside Maple and Brick. Five years had passed since their "final test," and the transformations that had begun in this small New Hampshire town had rippled out across the nation in ways none of them could have imagined.

Today was a day of celebration and reflection. Maple and Brick was hosting its first "National Innovation Summit," bringing together representatives from the dozens of innovation hubs that had sprung up across the country, inspired by their model.

As Bob watched the attendees file into the newly expanded conference center – once an abandoned warehouse, now a gleaming symbol of Peterborough's rebirth – he felt a profound sense of pride and humility. The parking lot was filled with cars bearing license plates from all over the country, a testament to how far their vision had spread.

"Quite a sight, isn't it?" came a familiar voice. Bob turned to see Alex Chen approaching, a warm smile on her face. Though she had long since transitioned from consultant to full-time executive at Maple and Brick, her keen insight remained as valuable as ever.

"Sometimes I can hardly believe it," Bob admitted. "Did you ever think, when we started this journey, that we'd end up here?"

Alex chuckled. "I knew we were onto something special, but this?" She gestured to the bustling scene before them. "This has exceeded even my wildest expectations."

As they made their way into the building, Bob's mind wandered back over the past five years. The decision to remain independent had been just the beginning. Freed from the threat of corporate takeover, Maple and Brick had doubled down on its commitment to innovation and community revitalization.

The open-source initiative that Jacob had proposed during their darkest hour had blossomed into a nationwide network of collaborative innovation. Small manufacturers, makers, and entrepreneurs from coast to coast were now connected, sharing ideas and resources in ways that were transforming the landscape of American manufacturing.

Emily's breakthroughs in sustainable materials had not only revolutionized Maple and Brick's product lines but had sparked a green manufacturing movement. The self-healing materials she had developed under pressure were now being used in everything from consumer electronics to critical infrastructure, dramatically reducing waste and extending product lifespans.

Joe, the once-skeptical veteran, had become an unlikely ambassador for their model of blending traditional craftsmanship with cutting-edge technology. His training programs, which taught experienced workers how to adapt their skills to new technologies, had been replicated in innovation hubs across the country.

Laura's marketing strategies had evolved into a broader mission of changing the narrative around American manufacturing. Through documentaries, social media campaigns, and partnerships with schools and universities, they were inspiring a new generation to see manufacturing not as a relic of the past, but as a high-tech, creative field full of opportunities.

As Bob and Alex entered the main conference hall, they were greeted by a sea of familiar and new faces. There was Mary, the former textile worker from Peterborough, now a respected expert in advanced manufacturing techniques. Mike, whose sustainable furniture startup had grown into a national brand, was chatting animatedly with a group of young entrepreneurs. Mayor Thompson from Millbrook was there too, along with mayors and community leaders from dozens of other towns that had established their own innovation hubs.

The buzz of conversation died down as Bob took the stage to deliver the opening address. Looking out over the crowd, he felt the weight of the moment.

"Welcome, everyone, to Maple and Brick's first National Innovation Summit," he began. "Five years ago, we stood at a crossroads. Our company, like so many others, was facing an uncertain future. But we made a choice – a choice to innovate, to reimagine what manufacturing could be in the 21st century, and to do so in a way that revitalized not just our company, but our community and beyond."

Bob went on to highlight some of the remarkable achievements that had sprung from their initiative. He spoke of the network of innovation hubs that now dotted the country, each one adapting the Maple and Brick model to its own unique circumstances and traditions. He talked about the renaissance in American manufacturing, with small and medium-sized enterprises leading the charge in sustainable, high-tech production.

"But perhaps our greatest achievement," Bob continued, his voice filled with emotion, "has been the rebirth of hope in communities that had been written off as casualties of globalization and automation. We've shown that with the right blend of innovation, education, and community engagement, small-town America can once again be at the forefront of manufacturing and technological advancement."

As Bob concluded his speech, the room erupted in applause. The energy was palpable as attendees broke into sessions, sharing best practices, discussing challenges, and collaborating on new ideas.

Throughout the day, Bob found himself marveling at the diversity of innovations on display. There was a group from a former coal mining town in West Virginia showcasing their breakthroughs in green energy storage. A team from a small city in Michigan presented their work on urban farming technologies. Representatives from a Native American reservation in Arizona demonstrated how they were combining traditional crafts with advanced materials to create unique, high-value products.

But it wasn't just the technological innovations that impressed Bob. It was the stories of community transformation, of renewed pride and purpose, of young people choosing to stay in or return to their hometowns because they saw a future there.

As the summit wound down, Bob found himself back outside, standing once again beneath the old maple tree. The setting sun painted the sky in hues of orange and pink, casting a warm glow over the Maple and Brick campus.

He was joined by the core team that had been with him from the beginning of this journey – Alex, Emily, Joe, Laura, and Jacob. They stood in comfortable silence for a moment, each lost in their own reflections.

"You know," Joe said finally, his gruff voice softened by emotion, "when we started all this, I thought you were crazy. Thought we were throwing away everything that made Maple and Brick special. But now I see – we weren't letting go of our legacy, we were building on it."

Emily nodded in agreement. "We've created something so much bigger than ourselves. Every innovation, every new hub, it's like we're planting seeds. And look at how they've grown."

"And we're just getting started," Jacob added, his eyes shining with excitement. "The collaborative network we've built, the ways we're combining different skills and technologies – the possibilities are endless."

Laura smiled, her marketing mind already whirring. "We're not just changing the way things are made," she said. "We're changing the way people think about manufacturing, about small towns, about the future of work."

Alex turned to Bob, a knowing look in her eye. "So, Bob," she said, "what's next? Where do we go from here?"

Bob looked out over the Maple and Brick campus, at the mix of historic buildings and modern additions, at the people streaming out of the conference center, energized and inspired. He thought about the journey that had brought them here, the challenges they'd overcome, the lives they'd touched.

"We keep growing," he said finally, his voice filled with quiet determination. "We keep innovating. But most importantly, we stay true to our roots. We remember that at the heart of all this technology and innovation are people and communities. That's our legacy, and that's our future."

As the team nodded in agreement, Bob felt a profound sense of gratitude and purpose. They had not just transformed a company or revitalized a town. They had sparked a movement, a rebirth of American manufacturing and small-town vitality.

The old maple tree rustled in the evening breeze, its leaves whispering of seasons past and seasons yet to come. Bob placed his hand on its rough bark, feeling connected to all those who had stood in this spot before him, who had faced their own challenges and dreamed their own big dreams.

"Well, old girl," he murmured, "looks like we've still got some growing to do."

As the team turned to head back into the factory, ready to start planning for the future, Bob took one last look at the scene before him. The legacy of Maple and Brick was no longer confined to these walls or this town. It lived in the renewed spirit of communities across the nation, in the bright eyes of young innovators, in the proud stance of skilled workers embracing new technologies.

They had not just adapted to the future; they had helped to shape it. And in doing so, they had written a new chapter in the story of American manufacturing – a story of rebirth, of innovation rooted in tradition, of technology guided by human values.

The transformation that had begun in one struggling factory had become a beacon of hope and possibility. And as the sun set on this day of celebration and reflection, Bob Harrington knew that the best was yet to come. The legacy of Maple and Brick would continue to grow, to inspire, to transform – one innovation, one community at a time.

CHAPTER 18 REFLECTION: REBIRTH AND LEGACY

Key Insights:
- ❖ The completion of a transformation is not an end, but a rebirth into a new phase.
- ❖ Our transformative journeys create legacies that can inspire and guide future generations.

Personal Reflection:
Consider the legacy you want to leave through your work or personal transformation. How are your current actions contributing to this legacy?

Application Question:
How can you ensure that the positive changes and lessons from your transformation continue to grow and evolve, even after your direct involvement ends?

Action Step:
Create a "legacy plan" outlining how you will document, share, and sustain the key learnings and achievements from your transformation journey.

Quote to Remember:
"Our greatest legacy is not what we achieve, but how we inspire others to transform."

CHAPTER 19: EPILOGUE

Five years had passed since Maple and Brick embarked on its transformative journey, and the factory in Peterborough, New Hampshire, was unrecognizable from the place it once was. The once-struggling company had not only survived but had flourished, becoming a beacon of innovation, sustainability, and community engagement.

Bob Harrington stood in the heart of the factory, now a vibrant hub of activity and creativity. The hum of machinery was accompanied by the chatter of workers discussing the latest project, and the air was filled with a palpable sense of purpose. The transformation had been difficult, but as Bob looked around, he knew it had all been worth it.

The Maple and Brick Way had become more than just an internal guide—it was now a recognized model for corporate transformation, studied by business leaders and academics alike. Companies from across the country, and even internationally, sought to learn from Maple and Brick's experience, eager to apply the same principles to their own challenges.

One of the most striking changes was the way Maple and Brick had integrated sustainability into every aspect of its operations. The development of the biodegradable polymer, once just a hopeful experiment, had revolutionized the company's product line. Now, Maple and Brick was a leading supplier of sustainable materials, with their products used in industries ranging from packaging to medical devices.

But the real success of Maple and Brick went beyond the products they created. It was in the culture that had been fostered within the company—a culture of creativity, innovation, and mutual respect. Cross-functional teams were now the norm, and ideas flowed freely across all levels of the organization. The mentorship program that paired seasoned employees with newer hires had not only preserved institutional knowledge but had also sparked a renaissance of ideas, blending the wisdom of experience with the energy of youth.

Bob's thoughts turned to the community outside the factory walls. The town of Peterborough had also experienced a revival, thanks in large part to Maple and Brick's commitment to local engagement. The factory had created new jobs and opportunities, but it had also invested in the community's future. Maple and Brick sponsored educational programs, supported local businesses, and worked closely with town leaders to ensure that the factory's success translated into broader economic growth.

The factory had even become a place of pride for the town, with tours regularly given to visitors who came to see the birthplace of the Maple and Brick Way. It wasn't just about showing off the advanced machinery or the latest innovations—it was about sharing the story of how a legacy company had found new life by staying true to its roots while embracing the future.

Bob smiled as he thought about the next generation of leaders at Maple and Brick. Many of the young people who had started their careers during the transformation were now stepping into leadership roles, bringing with them the lessons learned over the past five years. The company's future was in good hands, guided by the principles that had seen them through their darkest days.

As Bob prepared to leave the factory floor, he paused to look at the old maple tree that still stood proudly outside the main entrance. Its gnarled branches, once a symbol of the weight of legacy, now represented something much more—a testament to resilience, growth, and the power of renewal. The tree had been there through it all, and just like Maple and Brick, it had weathered the storms and come out stronger on the other side.

Bob knew that it was time for him to take a step back. The company no longer needed him at the helm—its success was now self-sustain-ing, driven by the people who had embraced the Maple and Brick Way as their own. As he walked through the factory one last time, Bob felt a deep sense of satisfaction and pride. He had fulfilled his duty to his ancestors, to the town, and to the generations of workers who had made Maple and Brick what it was today.

The future was bright, not just for Maple and Brick, but for everyone who had been part of its journey. The company had become more than just a business—it was a living example of what could be achieved when creativity, innovation, and community came together. The Maple and Brick Way was no longer just a set of principles; it was a legacy in its own right, one that would continue to inspire and guide for years to come.

As Bob walked away from the factory, the lights glowing warmly in the evening dusk, he knew that Maple and Brick's story was far from over. It was just the beginning of a new chapter, one that would be written by the hands and hearts of those who believed in the power of transformation.

CHAPTER 20:
THE MAPLE AND BRICK WAY

The transformation of Maple and Brick was not merely a story of survival; it was a rebirth, a renaissance of a company that had once been the heartbeat of a small New Hampshire town. Bob Harrington had always known that the path they were on was fraught with challenges, but what he hadn't fully grasped until now was how this journey would forge something much larger than a business turnaround.

As the years passed, the lessons learned, the battles fought, and the innovations pioneered at Maple and Brick coalesced into something more profound. It was no longer just about modernizing a factory or saving jobs—it had become a blueprint, a model for how any organization could transform itself in the face of overwhelming odds.

They called it "The Maple and Brick Way."

It wasn't just a set of principles or guidelines scribbled down in a corporate handbook. The Maple and Brick Way was born out of the real, gritty experience of pulling a legacy company back from the brink of collapse. It was an ethos, a culture, and a commitment to values that transcended profit margins and market share. It embodied a deep respect for the past, a fierce dedication to innovation, and an unyielding belief in the power of creativity.

Bob often found himself reflecting on the journey that led them here. He remembered the early days of doubt and resistance, the sleepless nights spent worrying whether they could really turn the ship around.

But he also remembered the sparks of creativity that kept them going: the moment when Emily proposed using nanotechnology to enhance their biodegradable polymer, the day Joe and Mike combined their knowledge to optimize the production line, and the countless brainstorming sessions that turned seemingly impossible challenges into new opportunities.

Each of these moments was a stepping stone, leading them not just out of crisis, but toward something new and vibrant. As Maple and Brick evolved, so did the people who worked there. They didn't just learn new skills or adopt new technologies; they embraced a culture of creativity and innovation, one that valued flexibility, experimentation, and collaboration over rigid adherence to the old ways.

It was this mindset that began to define the Maple and Brick Way.

Looking out over the factory floor, now humming with the rhythm of a company revitalized, Bob felt a profound sense of pride. This wasn't just about him, or even his family's legacy—this was about the people who had come together to create something new out of something old. The Maple and Brick Way wasn't a dictate from the top; it had been built from the ground up, forged in the fires of crisis and tempered by the hard work and ingenuity of everyone involved.

He recalled the moment when they decided to name this approach. It was during a late-night strategy session with Alex Chen, their transformation consultant, and a few key team members. They had been discussing how to ensure the lessons they were learning wouldn't be lost, how to codify the strategies and principles that were driving their success so others could learn from their experience.

It was Joe who had first uttered the phrase. He had leaned back in his chair, arms crossed, and said, "We're not just doing this for us. We're building something here—a way of doing things that honors where we've come from, but isn't afraid to push forward. It's the Maple and Brick Way."

The phrase stuck. From that moment on, it became shorthand for everything they were striving to achieve. It was a reminder that their transformation was not just about changing processes or updating technology—it was about creating a sustainable, forward-thinking culture that would carry the company into the future.

But what exactly was the Maple and Brick Way? What were the principles that guided them through the toughest of times and led them to where they stood today, stronger and more resilient than ever?

As we delve into the Maple and Brick Way, you'll discover the strategies that guided their remarkable journey—strategies that, when applied with care and commitment, can help any company find its own path to a brighter, more resilient future.

CHAPTER 21:
THE BLUEPRINT

The transformation of Maple and Brick was not just a story of survival; it was a rebirth, a renaissance of a company that had once been the heartbeat of a small New Hampshire town. As the years passed, the lessons learned, the battles fought, and the innovations pioneered at Maple and Brick coalesced into something more profound. It was no longer just about modernizing a factory or saving jobs—it had become a blueprint, a model for how any organization could transform itself in the face of overwhelming odds.

They called it "The Maple and Brick Way."

This wasn't just a set of principles scribbled down in a corporate handbook. The Maple and Brick Way was born out of the real, gritty experience of pulling a legacy company back from the brink of collapse. It was an ethos, a culture, and a commitment to values that transcended profit margins and market share. It embodied a deep respect for the past, a fierce dedication to innovation, and an unyielding belief in the power of creativity.

1. Honor the Past, Innovate for the Future

Principle: Leverage the strengths of your legacy while remaining open to new ideas and innovations. This balance between tradition and progress ensures that change is rooted in the company's core values.

Anecdote: The turning point for Maple and Brick came during a meeting between Joe, the veteran machinist, and Mike, the young engineer. Initially, their approaches clashed—Joe, with his decades of experience, was wary of the new automated systems Mike proposed. But as they worked together on the production line, they found a way to integrate the old with the new. Joe's deep understanding of the machinery, combined with Mike's fresh ideas, led to the development of a hybrid manufacturing process that enhanced both efficiency and quality. This breakthrough wasn't just technical; it symbolized the essence of the Maple and Brick Way—respecting the past while embracing the future.

2. People-Centered Leadership

Principle: Prioritize the well-being, development, and creative potential of your employees. People are the most valuable asset in any transformation, and fostering their creativity leads to continuous innovation.

Anecdote: During the early days of the transformation, tensions ran high. Employees were unsure of their place in the new Maple and Brick. It was during one of these uncertain times that Bob Harrington initiated the mentorship program, pairing experienced workers like Sarah with newer hires. Mary, once a textile worker, took a young recruit under her wing. Together, they experimented with new materials, blending Mary's hands-on experience with the recruit's technical knowledge. This partnership not only revitalized Mary's career but also led to a breakthrough in advanced manufacturing techniques that positioned Maple and Brick as an industry leader. The experience showed that when people are valued and their creativity nurtured, innovation naturally follows.

3. Sustainability as a Core Value

Principle: Commit to sustainable practices as a core business strategy, not just a trend. Sustainability should be integrated into every aspect of the business, with creativity playing a crucial role in finding innovative solutions that meet these goals.

Anecdote: Emily and her R&D team faced immense pressure to develop a new product line that aligned with the company's commitment to sustainability. After countless trials and setbacks, they finally succeeded in creating a biodegradable polymer enhanced with nanotechnology.

This innovation not only reduced the environmental impact of Maple and Brick's products but also opened new markets and strengthened the company's reputation as a leader in sustainable manufacturing. The key to their success was a relentless commitment to sustainability, coupled with the creative freedom to explore uncharted territories in material science.

4. Community Engagement

Principle: Recognize and embrace your company's role in the broader community. Strong community ties can be a source of strength and resilience during tough times, and engaging with the community can inspire creative solutions to shared challenges.

Anecdote: When word spread that Maple and Brick might be acquired by a corporate giant, the towns of Peterborough and Millbrook rallied around the company. Local businesses, schools, and residents organized a grassroots campaign to show their support, flooding the board with letters and packing town halls. This outpouring of community support wasn't just about saving jobs; it was about preserving the soul of the town. Maple and Brick responded by deepening its community engagement, sponsoring educational programs, and supporting local businesses. The strong bond between the company and the community became a cornerstone of their resilience, proving that businesses and communities thrive together.

5. Resilience and Adaptability through Innovation

Principle: Build a culture that is not only open to change but sees it as an opportunity for creative problem-solving and innovation. Resilience comes from the ability to adapt to new circumstances and pivot when necessary, using creativity as the engine for continuous improvement.

Anecdote: The decision to open-source some of Maple and Brick's technologies was born out of necessity during a time of intense competition. Jacob's idea to share certain innovations with the broader maker community seemed risky, but it turned out to be a masterstroke. The open-source initiative not only fostered collaboration and innovation but also created a network of independent innovation hubs that strengthened Maple and Brick's market position. This willingness to adapt and experiment with new ideas, even in the face of uncertainty, became a defining feature of the Maple and Brick Way.

Final Call to Action

The Maple and Brick Way is not just a story of one company's survival—it is a blueprint for transformation that any organization can adapt to its unique circumstances. The principles of honoring the past, prioritizing people, committing to sustainability, engaging with the community, and fostering resilience through innovation are universal. They provide a framework for navigating the complexities of modern business while staying true to core values.

Reflection: As you reflect on your own organization, consider how these principles might apply. What aspects of your legacy are worth preserving? How can you foster creativity and innovation within your team? Are you committed to sustainability, not just as a trend, but as a core value? How are you engaging with your community to build resilience? And most importantly, how are you preparing to adapt and innovate in the face of future challenges?

Action Step: Take a moment to assess your current strategies and practices. Identify areas where you can apply the Maple and Brick Way to strengthen your organization. Conduct a team workshop to explore how these principles can be integrated into your daily operations, decision-making processes, and long-term planning.

Quote to Remember: "The Maple and Brick Way teaches us that the most enduring transformations are those that honor the past, embrace the future, and place people at the heart of innovation."

By applying these lessons to your own journey, you can create a legacy of resilience, innovation, and community impact that will endure for generations.

www.ingramcontent.com/pod-product-compliance
Lightning Source LLC
Chambersburg PA
CBHW020427220526
45464CB00002B/592